DELE

ANYTHING IS POSSIBLE

ANYTHING IS POSSIBLE

Be Brave, Be Kind
& Follow Your Dreams

GARETH SOUTHGATE

with MATT WHYMAN

CENTURY

For any young person who is ever uncertain, confused,
or doubts themselves and thinks they're the only one feeling
the way they do. I hope you find something helpful,
comforting and inspiring within this book.

Contents

If I may say so, it is wonderful to know that this inspiring book by Gareth Southgate will make a huge difference to the lives and futures of young people across the country.

As the founder of The Prince's Trust over forty-four years ago, I have long been concerned that far too many young people in this country lack the confidence and skills needed to achieve their full potential. It was in the 1970s that I began to wonder whether, in some small way, I might be able to help, by providing personal development opportunities for young people and to empower them to get their own initiatives, or business ideas, off the ground.

My Prince's Trust gives young people the opportunity to change their lives. We believe that every young person should have the chance to succeed. As I have met many of these young people over the years, I have seen the transformational difference which can be achieved.

Books such as this are of critical importance as they offer expert help and advice for more young people. I am, therefore, immensely grateful to Prince's Trust Goodwill Ambassador Gareth Southgate, who has so generously supported my Trust for over fifteen years.

Many young people today face challenges and can endure setbacks, but they still have enormous potential. By believing in them, giving them crucial teamwork and leadership skills and supporting them to thrive, we can help them to succeed and society to prosper.

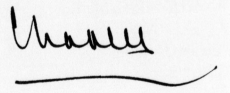

Introduction

If I can go from a skinny, introverted teenager who was once told he wouldn't make it as a footballer to someone who played for and managed his country, then I'm a clear example that *anything is possible*.

Football became the centre of my world at a very young age. My earliest memories involve kicking a ball around, either on my own or with my grandad in the park. If a football wasn't available, I'd use a tennis ball or even a stone. I'd play in the garden at home, in the street with other kids, or in my room with a soft ball. We did PE in my first years at primary school, but sadly football didn't feature. In those lessons, we spent most of our time getting into our gym kits before practising a bit of balancing or climbing up a rope. It was when I turned eight that I had a chance to play in proper games, and I loved it.

Football was my passion, pure and simple. As a boy, though I had no real understanding of the journey that lay ahead, I knew what I wanted to do with my life.

ME

That's how I started out, but each of us is unique. We all have different interests, qualities and personalities. We also have different hopes and dreams. What's more, not everyone has a clear vision for their future. That's perfectly normal, and no reason to worry. While some people might set themselves a goal at an early age, others find it takes time and life experience before they figure things out. There's no rule book, but the fact is we all have the potential to achieve great things. With the right mindset, preparation, guidance and support, a whole world of opportunity can open up for anyone, which is what this book is all about.

Today, as the England manager, I aim to focus with my players on what we can do to the best of our abilities, instead of worrying about what might go wrong. This doesn't just apply to football, but any goal we set ourselves – from passing an exam to literally shooting for the moon. Whether we're making a fresh start or just trying to be better at something, we all face challenges. This book aims to provide you with all the strategies and tools you need to make great things happen.

Along the way in life, there will be high points and low moments. You might even question if you've made the right choices, and think about giving up. As difficult as it might be to recognise in those tough times, it's all a learning experience that will benefit you in the long run. As proof of this, let me share my story . . .

In 1996, I played for England in one of our biggest games in thirty years. We had reached the semi-finals of the European Championship at Wembley Stadium. Only Germany stood in our way of a place in the final, but after ninety minutes and extra time, the score remained level at 1–1. It meant a penalty shoot-out would decide which team would go through.

At that time, penalties weren't something we practised much as a national side. We had great coaches, but it was seen as a matter of luck more than skill. With England and Germany level after five shots each, we were into the sudden death round. It meant the next side to go one goal up would win. All our obvious penalty-takers had taken a turn, and I was asked to take the next shot. I didn't say yes because I felt I was good at penalties. I stepped up because, having been the captain of almost every club I'd played for, I was used to taking responsibility.

Football is a team sport. Normally, I'm one of eleven players on the pitch. Just then, having positioned the ball and walked back a few paces, I felt all the attention on me. Rather than focus on the things I could control, like my breathing or what side of the net I should aim for, I started worrying about what might go wrong. *What if I slice the ball*, I fretted to myself, *or don't hit my target?* As a result, when the referee blew the whistle for me to take that penalty, my head was full of negativity.

On my run-up, I just focused on connecting with the ball. I didn't think about power or precise placement. In fact, I didn't really feel in control of my legs, and I definitely wasn't thinking clearly. As a result, I watched in shock and dismay as the keeper saved the shot. In that moment, I wanted the ground to swallow me up. I knew that if our keeper saved the next attempt from the opposition, then we could salvage things. Unlike me, however, the German player struck the ball with purpose past our goalkeeper David Seaman to win the shootout.

It was all over. The nation had been riding a wave of good feeling throughout the tournament, and that came crashing down with one kick. We had lost, and I felt completely responsible. Back in the dressing room, I carried a feeling that would stay with me for years. As I saw things, I had let everyone down: myself, my team and my country.

Returning home the next day, I just couldn't face anyone but my family. It was a bleak time. I felt anxious and nervous, as I didn't know how others would react to me. Nowadays, players have access to experts who can help them come to terms with difficult experiences like this. Back then I just had to find a way to deal with it myself.

The first thing that helped me was the messages I received from the general public. People wanted to let me know how much they'd enjoyed the tournament and that England had done so well to get to the semi-finals. They urged me not to blame myself for missing the penalty. It was just one of those things, they said.

Then there were the notes from incredibly brave individuals which touched me deeply. Some were living with terminal illnesses, or were devoted to caring for family members who relied on them. Despite this, they had taken the time out to write and thank me for playing a role in what had been such an exciting tournament for England.

This put everything into perspective. There I was, fretting about missing a penalty, when others had really serious issues to deal with in their lives. It was time I faced up to what had happened, and made the most of the future ahead of me.

Twenty-two years after that fateful night at Wembley, I found myself facing another England penalty shoot-out. This time, I wasn't one of the players; I was the team manager.

We had reached the knockout stage of the 2018 World Cup in Russia. A last-minute goal from Colombia had taken us into extra time. After thirty minutes of additional play, both teams remained level. It meant we now faced the final way of deciding who would go through, and what could seem like a cruel defeat for one side. I was well aware that it looked like

history might repeat itself. If England crashed out, I would be the man who lost it for the country as a player and now as a manager.

This time, however, I had faith in our preparation.

Over the years, I had spent more time than most thinking about penalty kicks. Whenever a game came down to this stage, we used to consider the result to be a roll of the dice. It was all about who had the courage to step up, rather than their skill or experience. This was one of the things I aimed to change when I took up the role of England manager in 2016. In fact, my experience in the Euro '96 semi-final had almost stopped me from accepting the job two decades on, because frankly I didn't want to get hurt again. But I managed to see beyond that, and with my coaching staff we worked hard with the players to practise something that was often left off the training schedule.

We viewed the penalty shoot-out just like any other challenge. With a positive approach, plenty of practice, and support for the players so they could improve and then master the skills, we went into that tournament with confidence in our ability to score in a shoot-out.

That night in Moscow, as players from each team took turns from the penalty spot, we focused on the process rather than the possible outcome. Only one side could win, of course, but I knew that we were relying on executing a skill under pressure rather than luck, which was down to the practice that we had put in during training. I was nervous, just like the players and the nation watching us at home, but this time it felt different. Watching the likes of Harry Kane and Marcus Rashford step up as planned, I knew we had done everything in advance to prepare for this moment.

AND WE WON.

I couldn't hide my delight, and pumped my fists with pride. The England team had taken ownership of their story, while I opened a new chapter in my life. Of course, I still wish that I had scored from the penalty spot as a player all those years ago, but I can honestly say that it changed me for the better. It was with this in mind that I consoled Mateus Uribe, the Colombian player who had hit the crossbar and paved the way for our victory. No doubt it seemed like the end of the world for him, but I knew it could also lead to a new beginning.

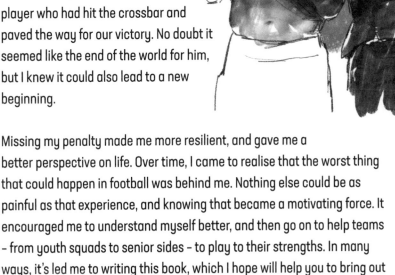

Missing my penalty made me more resilient, and gave me a better perspective on life. Over time, I came to realise that the worst thing that could happen in football was behind me. Nothing else could be as painful as that experience, and knowing that became a motivating force. It encouraged me to understand myself better, and then go on to help teams – from youth squads to senior sides – to play to their strengths. In many ways, it's led me to writing this book, which I hope will help you to bring out the best version of yourself.

Every single one of us has a life story to tell. Sometimes there are moments in it that don't work out as we'd hoped, or bring unexpected twists and turns. Then there's self-doubt and anxiety, which can creep in when things aren't going well and tempt us to give up. What matters is how we respond to these moments, and whether we turn them into learning opportunities. I hope that this book will help you to develop the qualities you need to tackle

THE BEST
VERSION OF
YOURSELF

new things in life, and I think you'll surprise yourself with just how much you can do.

We'll kick off by working out what makes us tick. Understanding ourselves is a key preparation before taking on any challenge. We need to identify our strengths, after all, but also recognise where there's room for improvement. Life is also about being brave, which often means stepping out of our comfort zone and testing ourselves.

We'll look at how working in teams can help us to be stronger together and inspire confidence. Even those who set out to achieve something special on their own require support, while leading by example can encourage others to step up when you need them.

With a positive mindset, a willingness to learn from our mistakes, and the ability to cope with both highs and lows, every one of us can make the most of our lives. It's about being brave, being kind and following your dreams.

So, if you're ready to turn the page, this is a chance to begin writing your story - and make it one that truly shines.

BE
BRAVE

Level
the
Playing
Field

What does bravery mean to you? We often think about it in terms of the kind of heroic act that earns a medal, but the fact is it's also something we can all harness to quietly improve our lives.

What we're talking about here is the quality we need to try new challenges. It's one that helps us step off the easy path in life and tackle something that seems difficult, or even impossible. We're likely to come across people who doubt that we can do it. We'll make mistakes, experience failure, and reach moments when it seems like we might never get there. When this happens, it's tough to learn from the experience and keep trying our best . . . but that's what being brave is all about.

Bravery doesn't always come naturally, of course. It exists in all of us, but we have to understand ourselves before we can bring it out. Then, when we're presented with a new goal or challenge, we can dare to take the first step.

Every professional footballer, including your heroes, will have a story to tell of setbacks and even rejection. I have never met a single player who sailed to success on the pitch. Even at a national level, you'd be surprised to learn how many players were released by a club in the early stages of their career. Then there are those who have suffered injuries that left them on the bench for long periods of time, or went through phases in which they simply underperformed.

In many ways, these challenges made the players who they are today. Overcoming difficulties and doubts will have helped them to grow tougher, wiser and more determined, but only they can truly appreciate just what they've been through to reach the top of their game.

For the fans watching a star striker beat two defenders before smashing the ball into the net, it's easy to forget that their success has been a long time in the making. When we only see the end result, it can seem as if that player must have been this good from the start. That's when we start comparing ourselves to them, and rule out any chance of following in their footsteps.

We all have people we admire for their achievements. Growing up, my hero was the Manchester United captain, Bryan Robson. At school, I started out playing in midfield like him. I would watch him on the television and try to move on the pitch like he did. When I grew out of my second pair of football boots, my dad bought me the same brand that Bryan wore. That made me feel really special.

I wanted to be like him in every single way, until slowly I found my feet and my own playing style. In many ways, heroes exist to spark a fire inside us. It's just important to recognise that they're also human.

MY HERO

Name: Bryan Robson

Role: Professional footballer and manager

Senior playing career: 1975–1997

Position: Midfielder

Played for: West Bromwich Albion, Manchester United, Middlesbrough, England

Playing characteristics: Speed, stamina, tackling, timing

Starting out: The son of a long-distance lorry driver, Bryan began his football apprenticeship at West Bromwich Albion in 1972, for a wage of £5 a week.

Career highlight: Bryan went on to become Manchester United's longest-serving captain, steering the team to two Premier League titles.

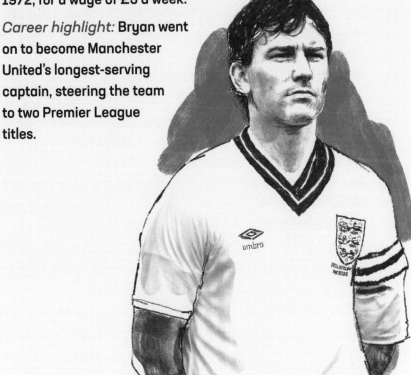

'WINNERS MAY SEEM TO BE LIVING THE DREAM, BUT THAT DOESN'T MAKE THEM SUPERHUMAN.'

In my new boots, I had no idea how hard Bryan Robson worked for the success he enjoyed. I just saw the winning goals and the glory. Fortunately, I had people around me who supported me in my ambition to become a professional footballer. They helped me to focus on taking one step at a time, and slowly build the determination I needed to deal with the difficult episodes all players have to go through. Without that help, I might well have looked at my hero and ruled out any hope of ever reaching the same league.

When it comes to sport, results are easy to see. Anything from a goal to a hole in one, or being first across the line on the athletics track or racing circuit, has a powerful impact. Yes, these winners are living the dream, but that doesn't make them superhuman. What we're actually seeing is the result of hard work and sacrifice which has often seen them put their lives on hold so that training could always come first - no matter what the weather. What's more, every one of them started out in the same place: with a passion for their chosen sport and an ambition to master it.

Right now, whatever your goals, that starting place is open to you too.

Growing up, I always thought of myself as totally normal. I loved kicking a ball around, just like many kids did, but there was nothing about me that marked me out as a future England player. I lived with my mum and dad in a nice house. It all seemed unremarkable at the time, but I recognise now how lucky I was - because my family life offered me stability and love. It's something everyone deserves to experience, a solid start in life, but the sad reality is that many miss out.

My dad had a job that sometimes took him to different offices around the country, and so we moved house a few times when I was young. Having started life in Watford, we headed for the north of England for a while, and then down to the south coast. It meant as soon as I got to know a few kids my age, we were off and I had to start all over again.

When it comes to meeting new people and making friends, we have to step out of our comfort zone. It can be awkward as you get to know each other and try to find common ground. That takes a little bit of courage, which didn't come naturally to me. But I had to do it, and those early experiences helped me to recognise that making an effort can bring rewards. I learned to adapt to new situations, socialise and fit in, which wouldn't have happened if I'd just stayed in my room.

As well as switching schools with every house move, and getting to know new classmates, I also had to start all over again with my football. Out on the street where we lived, in the schoolyard or the park, that meant getting to know a whole new set of young players and find my place among them. Sometimes this made me feel anxious - which is a natural response when facing a new situation - but the more I did it, the easier it became. When we moved to Crawley in West Sussex, where my family finally settled, I soon found another group of kids who shared my interest in the game. With a ball to kick between us, any awkwardness I felt quickly melted away. I discovered that football could help me to socialise and make friends.

Without a doubt, by the time I turned eight I was passionate about the game. I had a hero in Bryan Robson, and when I knocked a ball against a wall in my back garden I would imagine myself playing for England, in the

same way others might imagine themselves running the 100 metres at the Olympics or landing on the moon. I certainly didn't have the skills to back up my enthusiasm. Nothing marked me out as a lad who would one day step out for his country at Wembley Stadium. Why not? Quite simply because I hadn't begun to develop as a player.

'ALL I HAD WAS AMBITION, WHICH IS AVAILABLE TO US ALL.'

All About Ambition

- We're talking about a determination to make a dream come true, even if we don't quite know how.

- From earning a place on the school basketball team to playing tennis at a professional level, at every stage our ambition is about aiming to be the best that we can be.

- We can have ambitions in sport, at school, at home, in our friendships and relationships, and in the workplace. We all want to make the most of life, after all, and earn respect for our efforts in the process.

- With the right attitude, help, support and advice, each of us can act on our ambition and potentially transform our lives for the better.

- We all have the right to dream, and to take steps to turn that dream into a reality.

As a kid with a ball in my back garden, all I knew was that I loved to play football. In fact, when it came to those early experiences playing the game, I wasn't even aware of the learning process. At break times and after school, I'd look for anyone with a ball. In these loose kickabouts with schoolmates and friends, I found the ability level was completely mixed. There was usually quite a wide age range, and everyone was at different stages of their physical development. While sometimes I would shine, it also meant there would be players in the game who challenged me. I was always playing for fun, but this gave me the chance to step up and improve.

At home, it helped that my parents liked sport. My mum and dad would sometimes let me stay up for *Match of the Day* on a Saturday evening, or we'd sit together and watch a televised tournament or a big international game. I supported Manchester United, and experienced the excitement of following my team from one season to the next. I also had a taste of heartbreak when they lost to Southampton in the FA Cup Final one year, and ended up bawling my eyes out. I just felt so connected to the game and all the dramas that played out on the pitch.

One summer holiday, I watched a coaching series for younger viewers which fascinated me. I also owned a video of classic moments from the World Cup throughout the years, and soon came to know the history of the game. Sometimes, as a treat, my parents would buy me a football magazine, which I read from cover to cover, and of course I collected stickers! I just got my football from whatever source I could find, and it all came together to light that fire in me.

With my ambition burning, I really wanted to get involved in organised games. My first taste was a six-a-side tournament with the Cub Scouts. When I turned nine, I joined a Sunday league. Strictly speaking, the team was for players who were three years older than me, which just made me all the more determined to improve my game. I was also desperate to play for my primary school, but they reserved that for the kids in their final year. That didn't stop me from standing on the sidelines during matches, hoping a teacher would look kindly upon me - though they never did. I just had to wait my turn, and when it came I seized the opportunity.

The more I played, the more I learned from the experience and from other players, but the true skills, commitment and discipline I'd need to make it as a professional had yet to come. My early years in football were just a starting point for me, and there was nothing remarkable about them. But in a world where anything is possible, every single one of us has to begin somewhere. More often than not, that place is really quite normal. I wasn't the only kid with a passion for football and an ambition to become a professional one day. Nor did my ambition guarantee that I'd find success.

'I WAS JUST WILLING TO FOLLOW MY DREAMS AND BEGIN TO WORK OUT WHAT IT WOULD TAKE TO TURN THEM INTO A REALITY.'

Out of Nowhere

We all recognise these three successful figures, but do you know how they started out?

- Hollywood actor **Leonardo DiCaprio** grew up in a poor, crime-ridden Los Angeles neighbourhood. It's claimed he auditioned over 100 times before landing his first role.

- As a single mother living in Edinburgh, Scotland, **J. K. Rowling** wrote her first Harry Potter novel in cafés while her young daughter slept beside her. The finished manuscript was rejected by many publishers before Bloomsbury offered her a small book deal. The rest is history.

- UK heavyweight boxing champion **Anthony Joshua** has a shining reputation as a humble and dedicated athlete. Growing up in Watford, however, early brushes with the law nearly finished his career before it began. He believes that boxing gave him a chance to start afresh, and he worked hard to become a success.

'IF YOU CAN DO WHAT YOU DO BEST, AND BE HAPPY, YOU WILL BE FURTHER ALONG IN LIFE THAN MOST PEOPLE.' LEONARDO DiCAPRIO

'STAY HUNGRY.'

ANTHONY JOSHUA

SUMMARY

When it comes to managing our ambitions, we have to look at our heroes in a realistic light. Otherwise, we risk thinking that somehow they've been marked out for greatness - which can put us off pursuing our own goals.

'WHEN SOMETHING IS IMPORTANT ENOUGH, YOU DO IT EVEN IF THE ODDS ARE NOT IN YOUR FAVOUR.' *ELON MUSK*

Yes, people have achieved amazing things - from Elon Musk, and his pioneering work with electric cars and reusable rockets, to Dina Asher-Smith, the fastest British woman in recorded history - but they've also worked incredibly hard for it. Success might come quickly for some, or it could be a lifetime in the making. One thing is for certain, however: it's never easy.

No matter how long it takes, people who find success in life often started out on their path with no particular advantage. Some may have experienced hardships, or faced other challenges they had to overcome to keep working towards their goal. Everyone is different, but often we have to create our own opportunities. Our physical shape can sometimes play a role when it comes to being good at activities like rugby or ballet, but in most cases there is nothing to stop us from going for it.

Anyone who has successfully pursued their ambitions will have plenty of tales to tell - of setbacks, doubts, mistakes and disappointments. They've also shown a level of commitment that might mean early starts, or missing out on fun stuff with friends or family.

In every case, no matter what their aim or ambition, they never gave up. No matter how tough or challenging things became, anyone at the top of their game has learned to make the entire journey a learning experience and will have become stronger as a result.

The best heroes are those who are role models to us. They have achieved something extraordinary, but we still relate to them. Ultimately, their experiences represent what is possible, and can inspire us to set out on our own journey. Wherever our ambition takes us, if we embrace the same spirit as our heroes show, then we'll look back knowing we tried our very best at all times.

'I BELIEVE IN BEING THE BEST WOMAN YOU CAN BE FIRST AND FOREMOST, AND THEN THE BEST ATHLETE.'
DINA ASHER-SMITH

Obstacles to Opportunities

By nature, I am an introvert. This means I can be on the quiet side, and tend to get my energy from time on my own. As a teenager, it meant I wasn't totally comfortable with big gatherings like parties, or even walking into a changing room full of players. I was always the one who kept my head down and hoped nobody would take the mickey out of me.

At the same time, there are plenty of people who thrive in this kind of environment. They're often classed as extroverts. While they might be bored or restless on their own, extroverts find it easy to chat and joke around with others, and are comfortable when the spotlight is on them.

There is no right or wrong here. Some people are just naturally more outgoing than others. We're all wired differently after all, and that's part of what makes us unique.

If we're hoping to pursue a dream or ambition, then it's vital that we understand ourselves first. And that's not just about working out what we're good at. While it's great to be able to play to our strengths, it's perhaps more important that we understand our weaknesses. That way, we have a chance to address them, and even turn things around so we don't hold ourselves back.

Personality Test

There are all sorts of ways to work out what makes you tick. Here's one to help recognise if you're naturally more outgoing or you prefer your own company. The truth is we're all a little bit of both, but it's still a useful tool when it comes to understanding yourself.

INTROVERT	EXTROVERT
Shy	Outgoing
Quiet	Outspoken
Thoughtful	Thinks out loud
Creates their own energy	Energised around others
Likes to watch and observe	Likes to get stuck in
Patient	Impulsive
Relies on a few close friends	Makes lots of friends

When we talk about obstacles to success, it's easy to think about things beyond our control. Maybe you head to the local pool for a training session to find it's closed for maintenance, or can't join a local summer football camp because it's fully booked. Whatever we might find standing in our way, there's always a means of overcoming it. Whether it's switching to a workout on dry land or finding an alternative camp that's further away and requires a bike ride to get there and back, determination and creative thinking can take us far.

But what about those obstacles we create for ourselves? We're talking here about aspects of our character that hold us back, and which can quickly persuade us to give up chasing a goal or a dream. These obstacles of our own making lurk in our own minds, and often come down to a lack of confidence in ourselves. As a result, we delay or ditch an undertaking because we don't feel good enough. Sadly, bailing out like this can further reinforce the feeling that we're not cut out to do remarkable things with our lives.

The good news is that by learning to understand our different qualities, including the things that may stop us from fulfilling our potential, we can learn to conquer our weaknesses and even turn them into strengths. So, let's look at some common character traits that can work against us - and the strategies we can use to overcome them.

Worries

What's the problem?

We all have worries to varying degrees, which is a way of describing how it feels to be anxious. Anxiety is a natural response to a difficult or stressful situation. Think of it as an internal alarm system - one that's triggered by our brains to signal that we need to focus on finding a way to deal with the matter at hand. This is sometimes no bad thing.

In some ways, a little anxiety can help us take the necessary steps to complete a task - whether it's revising for exams or learning lines for a school play. The most effective way to deal with a worry is by acting on it, after all.

It can become a problem, however, if those worries won't go away, or if you find they kick in over the slightest thing. When this happens, turning your attention to a goal or ambition can be a trigger for stress, sleepless nights, and even physical symptoms like dizziness and nausea. Mild worries and anxiety can make it tempting to put your goal off or even abandon your idea completely; severe anxiety can affect your whole life.

What's going on?

In sounding the alarm bell over a worry, a fright or a stressful situation, the brain sends a signal to the body to release a natural hormone called adrenalin into the bloodstream. This can raise our heart rate and quicken our breathing, and it's designed to trigger a 'fight or flight' response. That's fine in the face of a physical threat, but not much use if you're dwelling on the fact that you might not perform well at an upcoming football trial. You can't fight a worry like that, or run away from it. As a result, the adrenalin can cause you to stew, and turn a minor concern into a crisis that literally leaves you feeling sick.

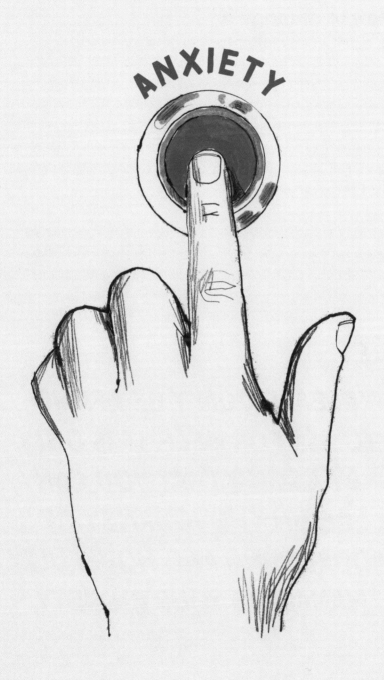

How to manage it

Not all anxiety can be overcome or managed without professional help. In severe cases such as generalised anxiety disorder (GAD), sufferers experience long-term anxiety that causes them to feel worried and concerned about a wide range of issues. People with GAD can feel anxious most days, and can struggle to remember when they did feel relaxed. If this sounds familiar to your daily life then check in with your doctor. Where appropriate, they can ensure you get targeted support, and work with you to find a solution.

However, if you are experiencing milder worries and anxieties, there are some broad steps that you can take that may help to ease your worries. Remember: we are all different, and this advice will not necessarily work for everyone. These are simply techniques that have worked for me. I want to share them in case they are useful for you.

'PLEASE DON'T BE AFRAID TO ASK FOR HELP. IT IS ONLY BY ASKING THAT YOU CAN BEGIN THE JOURNEY OF ADDRESSING AND HOPEFULLY MANAGING YOUR ANXIETY.'

- **Talk things through.** Opening up to someone you trust can give you some perspective. By putting your worries into words, chances are it won't seem so bad. Talking also helps you to feel that you're not alone in dealing with the situation.

- **Recognise the triggers.** Learning to identify that moment when your adrenalin levels rise means you can take yourself out of the situation for a while when or even before it happens. Rather than brooding alone with a worry on your mind, go for a walk and get some fresh air. It will help to burn off the adrenalin, and the change of scenery will give your mind some time out.

- **Make a list.** Writing down your worries can work wonders. Add a list of actions you can take to remove those worries from your mind.

- **Get stuck in.** It's natural to feel nervous before attempting something new. With no previous experience, everything is unfamiliar and it's hard to know how you'll feel or how well you'll perform. I'm not a natural public speaker. The first time I had to stand up and talk in front of an audience, I was worried. The next time wasn't quite so challenging – and the more I did it, the easier it became.

- **Own your worries.** Nerves are natural, and keep us on our toes. At the same time, you'll quickly put that feeling behind you by stepping out of your comfort zone and making that new place a familiar territory.

- **Create winning habits.** The more you deal with a worry successfully, the easier it is to manage worries in the future. By dealing with anxieties when they happen – whether you're talking things through with others or creating an action plan and putting it into practice – you'll find they no longer rule your life. A constructive approach like this will help you to feel calmer and more organised, two winning features when it comes to pursuing personal goals.

Fear of Failure

What's the problem?

Everyone has moments of self-doubt. Even the very best football players sit in the dressing room before a big game and wonder how they'll perform. It's a question that quickly leads to the thought that they might let their team down. Knowing how to process that moment of uncertainty constructively before they step out onto the pitch is vital. Otherwise, they risk losing their focus and may even live up to their worst fears.

Challenges are intended to test us. We face them in sport, at school, at work and in our personal and social lives. Whether we're taking an exam or asking someone out - or leading a team in the FA Cup Final - there's always a chance we might not be successful. It motivates us to prepare so we can give it our best shot, but sometimes that fear can grow in our minds until it threatens to overwhelm us.

What's going on?

A fear of failure can stop us from even attempting to succeed. In class, when the teacher asks a question, we've all been reluctant to put up our hand in case we're wrong. We worry that our classmates will judge us somehow. We think to ourselves that they might look at us, or even laugh . . . The trouble is, if we don't have a go and recognise that there's no shame in making mistakes, we'll never learn and get better.

The fact is we all want to succeed in the things we do. Nobody sets out to fail, but it happens. If all challenges were easy, or we knew all the answers in class, life would quickly become very dull indeed.

Challenges of any kind are a way of measuring our capabilities. They reveal a great deal to us about ourselves, and encourage us to improve in order to achieve. That's part of the draw when it comes to setting goals or pursuing ambitions. The journey we have to go on often requires us to learn about ourselves, master new skills and also deal with setbacks. We can't expect to succeed on the first attempt each time. So when we make mistakes or experience disappointments, or even fail in our attempts, it's important that we turn these moments into learning opportunities.

How to manage it

Everyone who has ever succeeded in life will have also experienced failure. It's part of the process, and it's an opportunity to come back stronger for the experience. Here's how to change the way you view mistakes and setbacks, so there's nothing to fear:

- **Whatever you're feeling is fine.** It takes courage to admit that you're frightened of failure. In some ways, recognising this in yourself is the first step towards overcoming it. The next step is to ask yourself what's fuelling that fear, because these are often factors you can actively address. If you tend to think negatively, for example, it's a matter of focusing on the positives in order to retrain your brain.

- **Consider all outcomes.** If failure is something you dread, it can feel like it's the only thing that will happen. But thinking negatively like this isn't going to bring out your best performance. If you go into an exam convinced it's going to be impossible, then you won't be prepared if it's easier than you think. Yes, there's a chance it might not work out, but there's always the possibility that you'll do well. Be ready for all eventualities.

- **Focus on the opportunities.** If you've given it your very best, then falling short or making a mistake is no reason to feel bad or ashamed. Of course, it can be disappointing, but it's also a chance to gain insight and knowledge. In some ways, it's the most effective way to improve. There might even be issues you need to address that only become clear when you try (and fail). Looking at it like this, often the only way to succeed is by making those mistakes in the first place. Recognising this is especially important for people who tend to get locked into the need for perfection right from the start, which is often impossible to pull off. If you focus only on perfection, all your early efforts will just bring disappointment and the temptation to give up. This is a shame, because every step of any journey is a chance to learn or get better at something.

- **Recognise the rewards.** Learning to deal with setbacks really is character-building. With a positive attitude, it can toughen you up and make you all the more determined to learn and then try again. When we see winners on the podium, part of their joy is down to the fact that they've also experienced the opposite feeling when things didn't go to plan. In short, earlier failures and mistakes make a success much more meaningful.

- **What's the worst that can happen?** If you're preparing for a challenge, focus on what it actually means if things don't work out straight away. Why? Because in reality, it's never as bad as you think. To go back to our earlier example, what if you answer a question in class and it's wrong? Are your classmates really going to laugh, or are they quietly going to rate you for putting your hand up when they didn't have the courage to do the same thing?

- **Failure is always a stepping stone to success.** This is about rethinking what setbacks and mistakes really mean. Many challenges and ambitions allow us to pick ourselves up, learn from the experience and try again. As a boy, David Beckham didn't get really good at keepie uppies overnight. It came down to years of practice, and constantly picking up the ball to start again. Even if it seems like we only have one chance to reach a pinnacle - like climbing a mountain or playing in a cup final - there will always be another opportunity if it doesn't work out as we hoped, even if it takes us in a new direction.

Confidence Crisis

What's the problem?

A lack of self-belief plays a role in almost every barrier we create for ourselves. Unless we feel confident in our abilities, we simply won't be in the right frame of mind to chase a goal or ambition. It's natural to feel a little nervous when we take on a new challenge, and question if we'll be successful. After all, we still have lots to learn on our journey. And as we pick up skills and experience along the way, so our confidence grows. But we still have to feel positive about ourselves before we set out. Otherwise, we can quickly convince ourselves that we're not good enough and give up.

What's going on?

People lack self-belief for all sorts of reasons. Our experience growing up can be a factor, because that's when we need people in our lives who believe in us so we can thrive. Comparing ourselves to others can also undermine our confidence. It's easy to focus on the successes other people experience – rather than the struggles they've been through – and feel like we'll never measure up. That sense that we're just not good enough can hold us back from living our lives to the fullest. It might be an intense feeling or just a nagging thought. In some severe instances, lack of self-belief can be connected to more serious mental health problems, such as clinical depression, when you can feel sad for weeks or months rather than days. In these situations, you should seek professional help and speak to your GP.

How to manage it

Overcoming confidence issues can make a huge difference in our lives. Even if some of us need extra or professional help to feel more positive about ourselves, we can all make small adjustments that might make a big difference:

- **Pinpoint a positive.** Aim to identify something about yourself that others notice, like and admire. It doesn't have to be much – maybe it's your sense of humour, your politeness or your smile. Just keep it in mind next time you're around people, because a good response can help you to feel better about yourself. Then it's just a question of building on that.

- **Upgrade your attitude.** If you're lacking self-confidence, it's easy to fall into a negative way of thinking. Consider how you respond to challenging situations such as a difficult piece of homework. Do you tell yourself you can't do it straight away, or do you give it your best shot? Remember that you might do better than you think, and making the effort will also leave you feeling better than you would by walking away from it, feeling like a failure.

- **Be around positive people.** Sometimes we can be held back by others without realising. It may even be a family member or a friend who simply doesn't understand your ambition. 'Why would you want to do that?' they ask, which can quickly undermine your confidence and drive. There's no need to cut these people out of your life completely. Just be aware that they can have a negative influence, and focus instead on those who believe in you and your goals.

- **Knowledge is power.** It's hard to feel confident when faced with a new challenge. As soon as we step out of our comfort zone, everything can feel unfamiliar or even threatening, which just leaves us feeling wobbly or small. However, if you spend time researching the challenge and learning more about it, it can become less intimidating, and there is a good chance that your confidence could grow. Whatever goal you have in mind, chances are there's a whole host of information about it online. You might also be able to speak to or connect with people who have already been through the experience. As you familiarise yourself with what's in store, your confidence can only rise.

- **Embrace mistakes**. Getting something wrong - or failing to perform as you'd hoped you would - is all part of a learning journey. It's not a reflection of your personal worth, or a sign that you'll never get it right. So, next time you make a mistake, instead of dwelling on any negative feelings, use it as an opportunity to figure out what went wrong and then work out how to do better next time. It's the surest way to learn from the experience, and you'll feel good about overcoming a hurdle.

- **Be bold.** How do you feel when you walk into a crowded room? No matter whether you're full of confidence or you're quiet and shy, chances are you suddenly become self-aware. *Am I dressed right? Who shall I talk to, and what do I say?* All manner of questions can rush through your mind - and that's completely normal! It's human nature to feel uncomfortable in some situations. What counts is how you act on this feeling. Leaving the room is the easy way out, but it won't make you feel better in the long run. The harder option is to take a deep breath and then introduce yourself to one or two people. Yes, it feels awkward, but by going in with a question and showing an interest in them, you'll quickly relax and find yourself chatting naturally. What's more, you'll come away having found the kind of confidence you didn't know you possessed.

Second Time Successful

Here are three famous names who experienced setbacks and failures before achieving their dreams:

- **Lady Gaga:** The *Born This Way* singer signed her first record deal with the Def Jam label, only to be dropped three months later. It shook her confidence but not her belief in the music she was creating, and her second record deal led to worldwide stardom.

- **Colonel Sanders:** The creator and face of KFC was fifty when he came up with his famous secret fried chicken recipe. Unfortunately, at first nobody shared his appetite for success. The Colonel is said to have visited more than 1,000 restaurants, cooking his chicken for the owners so they could taste it for themselves, before one agreed to go into business with him. Not much more than a decade later, KFC had become the sixth-largest restaurant chain in America.

- **James Dyson:** The man who reinvented the vacuum cleaner used up his life savings to create more than 5,000 prototypes over fifteen years, before finally coming up with the model that would make him a billionaire. We're talking about a lot of failures - but also one success that made it all worthwhile.

'IF YOU HAVE A
DREAM, FIGHT FOR IT'
LADY GAGA

SUMMARY

We've looked at common reasons why people delay pursuing their dreams, or even give up on them completely. Often, those reasons are found within us, and stem from a fear of failure or a lack of self-belief. That means we each have the power to address these sometimes-difficult personal issues and overcome them. Help is always available if we need it - ranging from a trusted friend to helplines dedicated to supporting young people - but ultimately it's in our own power to remove these obstacles.

It takes courage to admit there are aspects of our personality that need shaping up. Recognising our strengths and addressing our weaknesses can be a challenging process, but the rewards are limitless. Doing so means we can set ourselves challenges and goals with confidence and a positive outlook. It doesn't guarantee success, of course, but it does take you on a learning journey that can only benefit you in positive ways.

Max Out Your Mindset

How do you respond to a new and difficult challenge? It's a question that all of us will answer in different ways. Much depends on what's involved, any previous experience we might have, and our reason for taking it on.

From pursuing something you're passionate about to preparing for exams, life is full of tests. Whatever you're facing, however, there is one thing within your control that will have a big influence on whether you fail or succeed – and that's your mindset.

Mindset Made Easy

- We're talking about our attitude towards challenges here, and how we view our abilities and expectations.

- As we grow up, we form patterns of thinking that will either hold us back or help us to develop.

- Are you the kind of person who instinctively thinks they're not good enough to step outside their comfort zone - or are you someone who enjoys learning how to master new things?

- Lots of different factors feed into establishing our individual mindsets, from our upbringing and our friendship groups to how well we understand ourselves.

- Mindsets can be changed, upgraded and fine-tuned, to help us become our best selves . . .

- Believing in ourselves, recognising that mistakes are a learning opportunity and acting on feedback can all help to create a mindset that will enable us to recognise that anything is possible.

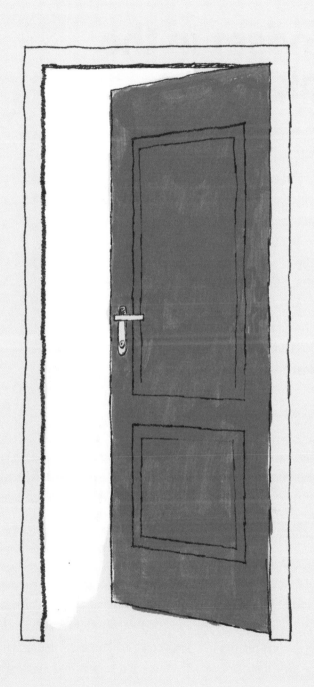

Mindset in the Making

Just as we develop physically, our mindset also grows over time. Everything we experience in life feeds into our attitude towards ourselves and the world around us. And it isn't just the high points and achievements which help us to feel confident and positive about our potential. Sometimes the low moments can teach us more about ourselves than anything else.

Growing up, I lived for football. It was fun, and the pitch was where I felt most comfortable. I also thought I was in good shape. I used to cycle to school, but I couldn't carry my school bag and my sports kit at the same time. So I used to ride home after lunch to pick up what I needed for training or a game in the afternoon or evening. I also enjoyed playing rugby and basketball, but knew that football was for me.

As a schoolboy, I started training one evening a week with Southampton. I was in the same year group as Alan Shearer, who would go on to play for Newcastle and England and become the Premier League's top goalscorer. They had a lot of good players - and as I was a late developer, many of them were bigger than me. I just did my best and hoped that I would catch up.

I was thirteen and a half when Southampton's Head of Youth Development wrote me a letter to say the club would be releasing me. They obviously thought I wasn't going to be good enough, and they even said they doubted I'd have the build. I was devastated. I'd spent two years training with them, watching the first team and hoping I could join them one day, and now that had come to an end. It was my first taste of rejection, and it left me in tears.

Around this time, I played football on a Sunday in Selsdon, near Croydon in South-East London. A lot of the boys were also training with nearby Crystal Palace. Once I'd got over the shock of being let go by Southampton, I wondered if there might be an opportunity for me there. I wanted to prove that Southampton had made the wrong decision, while also showing that I could still be a professional player. Having been knocked back so early in my journey, I found myself responding because of a mixture of negative and positive drivers. I am still motivated by a combination of these two elements, but this was when I began to understand how I deal with challenging situations.

I was thrilled when Crystal Palace took me on. I was fifteen years old and they invited me to play for the under-18 side. One year later, the club offered me an apprenticeship, with a small wage plus travel expenses from my home in West Sussex. It meant I faced a choice. After taking my O levels (now known as GCSEs), I could stay on at school for my A levels or follow the chance to work through the Palace youth and reserve squads, and finally earn my place as a first-team player.

It was a no-brainer. I'd been playing well that year, and thought I would just adapt to the step up from schoolboy to apprentice.

But I hated it.

All of a sudden, the game I played for fun became my work, and I found that I was treated differently. As a schoolboy, there had been no pressure. Playing up two age groups, I had always been the young one who was doing well. Southampton hadn't worked out as I'd hoped, but I was a little older when I started the apprenticeship at Palace and also bigger. Even so, I found the training became much tougher. As a full-time footballer, I was nowhere near strong enough. Early on, we had to do a twelve-minute circuit run. On my first attempt I was lapped by some of the older apprentices. The coach responded by making me do an extra lap. By the time I got over the finish line, I was blubbering.

While training became more challenging, my days were also longer; I had to catch two trains to travel between home and the grounds. It meant setting out first thing in the morning and not getting back until late. As an apprentice, I had to mop changing room floors, clean the toilets and look after boots belonging to the first-team players. I didn't mind hard work, but I struggled with the change from being a schoolkid to a young adult with responsibilities.

Then there were the difficulties I faced in terms of fitting in. I found a lot of the apprentice players around me were brimming with confidence. Being the quiet one, it meant I really stood out in the group. I didn't help myself on my first day of training. As a younger player, I was used to wearing smart clothes to travel to matches, and so I just thought everyone would dress that way for training. So I wore my school shirt and trousers, only to find when I arrived that everyone else was in a tracksuit or jeans. Cringing to myself, it felt like a disaster before I'd even started. All my peers seemed so much more streetwise, and I was just this kid from the suburbs with goofy teeth.

Nothing about me was cool, and I felt like I'd never fit in. On the pitch, surrounded by players who were used to a high level of training, I no longer felt like I could shine. I even began to pick up little injuries from trying harder. When I played in defence for the youth team we lost five of the first seven games, but I made a friend in the goalkeeper and bonded with him over the fact that we had let in 28 goals. Soon after that, I suffered an injury that meant I couldn't play the next game. The coach, Alan Smith, called me in for a chat and just spoke his mind.

'You weren't going to play anyway,' he said. 'You're a lovely bloke, Gareth, but as a footballer you've got no chance. If I were you, I'd think about becoming a travel agent.'

I realised later that Alan wasn't really letting me go. He was just looking for a reaction. It was his way of waking me up to the fact that I needed to make some serious changes to my outlook and commitment if I was going to survive. But at the time, I left and just cried my eyes out.

One of the older players took pity on me and gave me a lift home. On the way, he talked to me about the realities of the professional game and how it worked. He could tell that all the fun had gone out of it for me, and that I had yet to feel comfortable in such a competitive and aggressive environment. Even so, he left me thinking that with the right mindset I could turn this low moment into a learning experience.

Without a doubt, it was a challenging start to my football career. I could've taken my coach's harsh words to heart and my dreams would have ended right there. Instead, despite feeling very sorry for myself, I knew what I had to do.

'IF I WAS GOING TO SURVIVE AND EVEN THRIVE IN MY APPRENTICESHIP, I NEEDED TO TOUGHEN UP. THIS IS A QUALITY THAT'S OFTEN CALLED 'RESILIENCE'. IF I HAD ANY CHANCE OF A FUTURE AS A PROFESSIONAL FOOTBALLER, I HAD TO FIND IT IN ME.'

Get Resilient

- Resilience is the ability to get through difficult or testing situations.

- People sometimes talk about 'bouncing back' or 'picking yourself up' after facing challenges and not being successful.

- We can think of resilience as an emotional suit of armour. It's there to protect us from getting hurt, and also allows us to get back on our feet to fight another day.

Resilience often comes from experiencing difficult moments in pursuit of a goal, and working out a way to stay on course. In my case, facing the real possibility that my footballing career was over before it had really begun, I knew that I had to get stronger - not just emotionally, but physically. I needed to do weight training to build muscle. I had to improve my running stamina. Looking back at the time I was lapped on that circuit run, I knew I could've pushed myself to go faster. It was the self-doubt in my mind that had held me back, and somehow I had to change my thinking to break free of that. At the time, I really didn't enjoy the pain that could come from training hard. I needed to find a way to turn that around, and see the discomfort as a sign that I had worked as hard as I could.

In short, I had to leave behind my time as a schoolboy footballer and adapt to becoming a professional. That meant having the right mindset and finding the resilience to see me through the long journey ahead.

Toughen-Up Tactics

- **Stay calm.** Even when things aren't going well, aim to keep a level head. It's fine to be emotional if you've suffered a setback or a loss, but look at it as part of the process rather than dwelling on it.

EVERY CLOUD HAS A SILVER LINING

- **Find a friend.** Talking through your experiences of a disappointment or challenging time can help you to make sense of the situation. It's better than bottling things up, which can give rise to feelings that will hold you back in the future.

- **Don't lose sight of your goal.** Some obstacles can seem impossible to overcome, but there is always a way.

- **Learn lessons, and strive to improve.** This is the surest way to keep progressing, and become stronger for the experience.

Finding Your Feet

We each have the power to shape our mindset and build resilience. It requires self-awareness, and can take time and experience, but what really helps is having people around who believe in you. Pursuing a dream or ambition can be a lonely journey at times, especially during the low moments. Knowing that someone has faith in you, or that you can confide in them at any time, can help to keep you focused and on track.

My parents were supportive, but not pushy – they knew how to nudge me at the right time. When my dad came to watch me as a schoolboy player, he didn't stand on the sidelines bellowing at me. He's always been a very humble guy, and I could tell that if I played well then he'd be quietly proud. On the drive home from a match, a lot of kids would find themselves stuck with a parent who interrogated them if they hadn't performed. My dad would just share a couple of pointers about where I could improve, and this constructive approach had a big influence on me. Rather than making me feel embarrassed, angry or awkward, it helped me to develop the mindset I needed for my journey.

My dad certainly helped me to feel good when I played well, while recognising that I could always learn and strive to do better. These little nudges were central to my early development. It was about creating space for me to find my own way, rather than piling on pressure. Instead of talking about my long-term goals before I really understood what was involved, he'd focus on more immediate matters, like asking if I'd been for my run. I never felt like Dad was pushing me to do something that he wanted. He knew I had a dream, and so he was just offering small reminders of what I needed to do to make it happen.

My mum supported me in a different way, but it was just as important to my development. When Crystal Palace offered me the apprenticeship, she made sure I worked hard at school to get some decent qualifications first. Together, my parents gave me the opportunities and confidence I needed to take my first small steps on what would be a long journey. This helped me to build the mindset and resilience I needed as I set out to become a professional footballer.

Believing in Yourself

Confidence comes from within. A positive attitude towards taking on new challenges - and a toughness to help us get through the rough patches - brings out the best in us all. It can help us to become more independent, and to recognise the road to success.

As a young footballer, there were definitely a few times when I didn't play well on a Saturday because I'd let my training slip during the week. I could see the connection between my actions and the outcome, and I would tell myself I had to do better. As I saw it, I needed to learn from these experiences rather than keep repeating them, and that attitude fed into my overall mindset. Over time, I found that when I made a gut decision, it was based on lessons I'd learned. This helped me to be more considered, rather than just doing something without thinking things through.

It's impossible to go through life without making mistakes. The harder you push yourself and the further you travel on your journey, the more likely you are to stumble or slip up. At the same time, I soon came to realise that if you can pick yourself up each time, then mistakes are basically a chance to make sure you don't repeat them. It's just a question of having the right attitude to act on what went wrong, and a desire to keep improving.

SUMMARY

It's never too late to rethink how you feel about your abilities and your potential to get better at something. Sometimes we can rule ourselves out of taking on challenges because our attitude lets us down. We might say we're not born to do it, or we lack the practice, but the fact is everyone has to start somewhere. What's more, even shining stars make errors along the way. If we can recognise this, and accept that becoming really good at something is a process that takes time, then we can go far.

In my early years as an apprentice at Crystal Palace, I constantly found myself around players with more speed or ability than me. Rather than let that undermine my confidence, I started to ask myself what I needed to do to play at the same level as them. This is an experience we will all go through when we're in any kind of talent programme. Just as we get good at something, someone else comes along who is better. So, do we give up - or do we take inspiration from them to improve?

'ULTIMATELY, HOW WE RESPOND
IS DOWN TO US, WHICH IS WHY
IT'S SO IMPORTANT TO HAVE
A POSITIVE MINDSET AND A
RESILIENT APPROACH.'

Dream On

Goals in life come in all sorts of forms. From short-term aims, like delivering a school project on time, to long-term targets such as training to become a professional rugby player or a doctor, mechanic or architect. Goals provide us with an opportunity to focus, and if they're challenging, that means learning new skills and mastering them through practice.

Some people have an idea of what they want to do with their lives from an early age. Others aren't so sure, and find it's something that takes shape over time. There is no set pathway, but it's easy to think you're missing out when it seems like everyone else has a plan for their future. The key is to keep an open mind. Sometimes things can seem beyond your abilities, which is when you have to remind yourself that anything is possible - if you're prepared to go on a journey.

So, whether you're dreaming big or simply hoping to turn over a new leaf in the classroom - or looking to improve any aspect of your life where you know you can do better - let's look at the process we all have to go through to make it a reality. Even if you have no goals in mind right now, you owe it to yourself to be ready to act when things start to take shape.

So Near, So Far . . .

My dream was to play for England. It was that simple. It had been my goal since I started kicking a ball about in the back garden as a boy. Of course, at that time, I had no idea of what it would take to make that happen. It was just something I kept thinking about, without really considering just how few players made it to the national squad, and it was a dream that never really left me.

I imagined myself in an England shirt when I first started playing organised games – from primary to secondary school, and then as an apprentice at Crystal Palace. I was acting on my ambitions, and learning to adapt to the increased demands. Even so, as I travelled further on my journey, my dream destination seemed further away.

Why? Because reality had set in.

As I got more involved in professional football, moving up at Palace to play with the reserves and even captaining the side, it became increasingly clear to me just what was required to reach the national squad. All the England players were quite literally at the top of their game. They had made themselves selectable by being exceptional, and the manager could pick from the cream of the crop.

Several years after starting my apprenticeship at Crystal Palace, I was called up to play for the first team. It was an honour, but we viewed ourselves as one of the smaller clubs. Palace were in the top division – this was shortly before the creation of the Premier League in 1992 – but at that time the players who wore the England shirt tended to come from major sides like Manchester United, Liverpool and Tottenham Hotspur.

I never lost sight of my dream, but I also recognised how far I'd come. Yes, it had been a struggle to begin with, but I had slowly learned to turn obstacles into motivating forces. I even enjoyed training hard, and looked back on Alan Smith's tough talk as a turning point for me. I had needed that wake-up call, even though it was difficult to take at the time.

'AFTER YEARS OF HARD WORK, I HAD BECOME A PROFESSIONAL FOOTBALLER.'

Then, at the end of a challenging time in the Premier League's first season, Crystal Palace were relegated. As a result, any hope I had that I might one day play for England pretty much came to an end. At the same time, Alan Smith took over as Palace manager. It was a great honour when he made me captain, but it was also daunting because I was only twenty-three, and other players on the team were older than me. Still, I was determined to prove myself – as was the entire team – and we finished the 1993–94 season by winning the First Division and returning to the top flight.

One year later, I moved to Aston Villa. It was another step up, because now I found myself on the pitch with international players. Once again, I had to adapt until I felt comfortable at this new level, and that's when my dream of playing for England came back onto my radar. Compared to many players who'd made their international debuts, I was in a relatively late stage in my football career, but I began to think the jump wasn't that big. If I continued to focus on playing to the best of my abilities, I hoped I would make myself selectable.

In my first season with Villa, late in 1995, I received the call-up I'd been dreaming about since I was a boy. I made my debut for England by coming on as a substitute in a match against Portugal. I'd had no idea what a rollercoaster ride lay ahead of me when I first imagined myself in an England shirt. Like any journey, my path had been marked by highs and lows. There had been difficult moments, when I'd questioned if I would ever make it this far, but every single experience played a part in my development as a player.

I'd reached that moment when I finally realised my dream came down to belief – and to working hard to meet the challenges I faced.

Dream Times

In the 1930s, a Swedish professor called Anders Ericsson looked into how long it takes to get really good at something. The theory was popularised by an author called Malcolm Gladwell, and states that it takes ten thousand hours of practice and experience for anyone to truly master a skill. So, if you've set your sights on becoming an elite player in any walk of life, here's what it could take to reach that magic number:

- Four hours a day, seven days a week, for a whole year, with Christmas off.

- Two hours a day, Monday to Friday, for the best part of three years.

- One hour a day for a little more than twenty-seven years.

Stages to Success

For years, I wanted to run a marathon. It's just one of those challenges that appealed to me. When the right time came for me to take on the 26.2 miles, I set out to follow a training programme. Why? Because at the start of that programme I was used to running no more than a couple of miles, something I did in training as a footballer. A marathon was completely different. At the time, the thought of running that kind of distance was hard to get my head around.

Had I tried without training and the proper preparation, I would have failed.

The aim of the programme was to slowly build up the distance as well as my fitness and stamina, so I felt comfortable with the increased mileage. It was a question of gently pushing myself – making sure I factored in rest to let my body recover – and just following the plan that would eventually see me take my place on the start line. The training programme took a few months to work through, but the experience of completing a marathon is something I'll never forget.

When it comes to facing something that seems impossible, and then making it happen, we all have to go through the same process. In order for it to become realistic, it's vital that we break down what's involved into smaller chunks. Otherwise our ambitions can seem so far away that it's hard to see how we'll ever get there.

If a mountaineer peers up at the summit from base camp, the climb they face might appear to be overwhelming. That's when doubts can creep in and quickly undermine confidence. To avoid this, the mountaineer will break the climb into stages. By focusing on completing one section after another, the task becomes manageable.

We don't have to be scaling a rock face to find this way of thinking useful.

On the marathon start line, I didn't think about the finish. Frankly, it was just too far away. Instead I concentrated on reaching each mile marker. It meant that, as I tired, the next goal didn't seem so far away, and this approach helped me to reach the end.

From mountaineering and marathon-running to working towards playing for your country or pursuing a career that takes multiple qualifications and years of training, we can make great things happen by breaking the journey into stages. It's a useful way to approach ambitions of any shape or size, no matter how long it takes to get there.

Ultimately, it means we can seriously consider big goals without thinking anything is beyond our reach. After all, astronauts started out with a dream of one day making it into space. Yes, it may have taken those dreamers years of research, specialist training, hard work and sacrifice before they even made it to the launchpad. There's no doubt it would have been a long and difficult journey, and yet the only way they could possibly set off was by establishing a plan of steps to reach their goal.

Creating markers is also a really effective means of measuring progress. Whatever goal we set ourselves - and it can be so much more or less than a marathon - it means we know how far we've come, and we know what's left until we reach our destination.

Dealing with Doubters

There will always be people who say it can't be done. Sometimes it's even the people closest to us. Here's how to respond constructively and maybe even transform them into supporters:

- **Listen to their reasons.** Even if that person has dismissed your dream outright, give them a chance to talk. It shows respect, and allows you to understand their point of view.

- **Respond constructively.** Often people cast doubt on big dreams if they believe you haven't thought things through. Addressing their concerns gives you a chance to show you're aware of what's in store, and have the attitude and resilience to cope.

- **Share your plan of action.** If you've broken down the journey into realistic stages, you might find that sharing your plan will invite useful input. Maybe you've missed something, or it sparks a discussion that allows you to test if the plan is in the best shape possible.

- **Welcome their support.** By now, your calm, positive and mature approach will have gone some way to winning them round. At the same time, stress what their blessing or backing for this undertaking would mean to you - even if they're just giving you a chance to talk when you need it.

- **Share your progress.** Keeping people posted can help them to become emotionally invested in your journey. By telling them about the highs and lows, the hard slogs and surprises, you might find that those who once said it couldn't be done become sources of support and positive energy.

The Making of You

We've seen how easy it is to look at people who have achieved success, and not appreciate the journey they've undertaken to get there. Another easy mistake to make is to compare yourself to others, which is also a sure-fire way to undermine your self-confidence. Playing football as an apprentice, I found myself on the pitch with a whole team who shared my hopes and dreams of becoming a professional or wearing an England shirt. At first, it seemed to me that they were better players. I would struggle to reach their level, and had to learn to adapt and improve.

We tend to notice those who excel, and then measure our performance against theirs. But no matter what field you're in - from sport to school and beyond - the most constructive way to be in competition is with yourself rather than anyone else. Here are some reasons why:

- You can't control how someone else performs.

- They might be further ahead on their journey than you.

- Some people might find certain skills easier to pick up.

- Other variables like age and maturity can be a factor.

- Physical build can also make a difference in various sports and activities.

With this in mind, imagine that you've devoted your life to becoming an Olympic sprinter. After years of tough training and missing out on time with friends and family, the opportunity arises. You're on the blocks, the gun fires. You run a personal best, the fastest time you've ever recorded . . . and come last.

Is this a failure? Far from it.

The fact is you worked hard to represent your country at the highest level. You competed against the best runners in the world, and while you didn't make the podium you still earned a PB. Not only could your efforts be a stepping stone on a longer journey – and lead to a chance to come back stronger from the experience – but you put in the performance of a lifetime (so far). It's a question of perspective, and it could make the difference between giving up on your dream because you don't feel good enough, and feeling like you've made progress and pushing on.

Being in competition with yourself first, no matter what your goal, will help you to make progress. At school, I was in the top set for maths. In truth, I should have been in the set below, because I struggled compared to the other kids. That didn't do much for my confidence. I passed the exam, though had I been in the right set, learning the same things but in a way that better suited my ability, I might have got a higher grade.

There are all kinds of ways we can help ourselves when taking on a challenge. One thing we can do before we've even begun is to focus on our own performance rather than those of others. Of course, it's tempting to look around at the competition, but what matters here is our journey. And that means placing ourselves in the right environment to learn the skills we need.

We're talking about small nudges here, rather than being hopelessly out of our depth in a bid to keep up with others. This approach creates momentum, rather than feeling like we're sinking, and gives us every chance of turning our dreams into a story of success.

SUMMARY

What drives us to pursue goals? Why do we step out of our nice comfort zones and set about what can sometimes be years of hard work before we achieve our dreams? It's an important question we need to ask ourselves before making the commitment. Because no matter what goal we have in mind, our drive for it has to come from the heart.

Praise is nice to receive when we reach our goals. It feels good if we've worked hard at exams, or emerged covered in mud from head to toe having completed an assault course. Even so, earning that recognition shouldn't be the main reason why we take on challenges in the first place.

When we consider the commitment required and the journey involved in getting really good at something, it's clear we have to be passionate about it. If I didn't love playing football, I might well have given up when things got tough as an apprentice. Passion is what helps us to stay focused on achieving our dreams, especially when we face a testing time. Even if we do find success in front of a stadium full of fans, the real reward comes from knowing how much work we put into reaching that moment.

So, in working out what goals to pursue, be clear about the driving force. Social media, for example, can make it easy to get recognition quickly. It can be a great way to showcase talent for an audience, and a useful tool for communication and receiving support in your journey towards achieving a dream or ambition. At the same time, an online platform can bring negativity and unwanted attention into your life, which could impact everything from motivation to mental health.

It's an individual choice, of course, but we owe it to ourselves to be aware of both the advantages and the drawbacks of pursuing our ambitions so visibly. Most important of all, if the sole aim of any goal is to impress others, then ultimately it's not going to provide lasting fulfilment. Chasing fame can seem attractive – but without real substance behind it, the spotlight will quickly move on.

Attention from others, or external approval, is no match for the fire inside us. That inner passion is such a powerful driving force when we're trying to achieve something special. Just be aware that sometimes on our journey there will be times where we're faced with doing things we don't love quite so much. A student doctor may not relish revising for a biology exam late into the night, which is why they have to remind themselves of their long-term goal.

So, before chasing any dream, we need to answer some simple questions: Do we believe in what we're about to undertake, with both heart and soul? Are we prepared to take on some short-term challenges that aren't much fun, because they'll help us achieve our long-term goal?

If so, with resilience and the right mindset in place, nothing can stop us from making it happen.

Ready?
Go!

There's nothing better than taking on an exciting new challenge, whether it's a lifelong ambition or a recent opportunity that's too good to overlook. All of a sudden, that goal can command the majority of our attention. It occupies our thoughts, and becomes the first thing we want to talk about. In most cases, we can't wait to get stuck in.

But it can also be a daunting time for us, filled with doubt and uncertainty. Partly, this is down to a fear of the unknown. If we've never experienced anything like the journey we're facing, it's only natural to question how it'll work out.

So, how do we know when the time is right to start that climb, run or rehearsal, and what do we need to tick off the checklist first? We each have to make our own decisions, of course, and sometimes it's a question of trial and error. Even so, there's plenty we can consider before taking that vital first step, to bring both confidence and peace of mind.

Right Place, Right Time?

Some challenges start with putting an event in the diary. It might be a match or an exam, and the date gives us something to work towards. We have time to get our heads around what's involved and prepare for that moment. Whether it's training programmes or revision plans, we need to make use of our time before the moment arrives to put ourselves to the test.

Then there are those challenges with no clear timetable. It might be something we've decided to do for ourselves, like starting a podcast or learning how to play the guitar. These are the goals that are easy to put off. Often, the time never feels right, or we start before we've properly prepared and quickly give up when it doesn't work out as we'd hoped.

And sometimes opportunities arise that we can't turn down, even if we haven't had time to fully adapt. When my playing career came to an end, after six years at Aston Villa and then five at Middlesbrough, I was offered the chance to take up the role of manager. It meant finishing my last season as captain, and then beginning the next in charge of everything from team selection, strategy and formation, to player transfers and staff responsibilities. I accepted the job based on my experience wearing the captain's armband. I was used to speaking to the team and knew how I wanted to be treated as a player. Looking back, that was nowhere near enough in terms of preparation for being club manager. I had no idea how complex it was going to be. It all happened so quickly, in fact, that I didn't take my coaching qualifications until after the season had started.

At first, my main concern was how my relationship with the players would change. But once I began, I realised there was a whole lot more to concern myself with. I had little understanding of a business organisation, and yet so much of the job demanded skills and experience in this field. Then there was the question of what kind of playing style I wanted to encourage, and how that might shape our training. There were just so many layers. With no previous experience in the job, it felt overwhelming.

That early stage of my career as a manager was stressful. In every situation I went into, I didn't really know the answers. I had to put on a front that I knew what I was doing, but I was doubting myself as I didn't have any evidence of what was needed to be successful.

Looking back now, I can appreciate that I learned a great deal about becoming the manager I wanted to be from gaining experience in the role. It was a difficult learning environment, however. Why? Because while I could learn from my mistakes, those errors could cost the team. At the same time, I couldn't turn down the opportunity to manage a club like Middlesbrough. I had to find my feet as fast as possible, but I was constantly learning throughout my time in the job.

Often, the right moment to take on a challenge is not clear-cut. The decision is down to the individual and their situation. Even if we lack the skills before we start, and need to go on the journey in order to pick them up, the one thing that will see us through is a clear understanding of ourselves and our objectives. That way, no matter how hard it becomes, we can be confident in saying that starting the journey was the right decision to make.

On Goals

There is an effective way to work out if the challenge we have in mind is right for us, and that's by writing it all down. Often, when we have a burning need to get stuck into something new or exciting, it can seem overwhelming. If there's lots to consider, then it's hard to make sense of it all. All manner of thoughts can whirl around in our minds, and that's when our aims and objectives can get lost.

Before setting our sights on a goal, we have to know why we want to achieve it and what it involves. What's our motivation, and the reward for our hard work? It might be a place on the first team, a qualification for playing a musical instrument or a role in the school play. Whatever's under consideration, use the space under these examples to help make sense of it all

CHALLENGE CHECKER

What's my goal? *to improve my 5K time from 22 mins to under 20*

What's involved? *training with the running club*

How much time will it require? *two one-hour sessions each week*

How long will it take? *6–8 weeks (review weekly)*

What do I need? *a new pair of running shoes*

Drawbacks? *must finish homework before each session and save for the shoes*

Advantages? *a PB!*

Kick Off with Confidence

Whether you have time to prepare for a challenge, or you're learning as you go, here's how to take care of yourself:

- **Create a support network.** Even if you're alone in pursuing your goal, it feels good to know that people who care for you are there when you need them. Whether it's a parent, a carer, a teacher or a trusted friend, you might find the challenges you're facing become easier once they're shared.

- **Talk to people who have undertaken your journey.** From a student in the year above who has sat their exams to a player from the next age group, or anyone who has mastered the skills you're hoping to learn, talking to someone who has been through what you're about to embark on can be a source of inspiration, guidance and support.

- **Help yourself.** We know the benefits of time spent practising a task or a skill. Even if a challenge may seem difficult to prepare for without actually doing it - such as learning to surf or roller-skate - there are still creative ways of preparing or improving that you can build into your normal routine, such as online video tutorials or fitness programmes designed to get you in the right shape.

- **Take time out.** It's important to look after yourself when pursuing any ambition. The step up in commitment, as well as the demands that come with learning new skills, can impact on your physical and emotional health. So, take time away from your task, in order to rest, recharge and be with those who care about your welfare.

Beware the Big Announcement

No matter what we want to aim for in life - whether it's short- or long-term - deciding on that goal is a moment we often find hard to keep to ourselves. We're setting ourselves up for a challenge that means doing something we enjoy, after all, or which will allow us to grow as an individual. Sharing our plans with people who have our best interests at heart is a healthy thing. We want to build that support network, after all.

But just be aware that there's a big difference between confiding in a good friend or family member and going public with your plans. Making a grand announcement might be tempting, but we have to ask ourselves if it's the right thing to do at this stage. We only have to imagine how our friends might react if we suddenly announced our intention to become prime minister or work on the International Space Station. Both are healthy ambitions, but they also involve very long journeys with lots of steps along the way. This is fine if we're passionate, committed and aware of what it takes to get there. But for those around us, it probably all just seems so far away and unlikely, and chances are they'd laugh.

Ask yourself if this response will be helpful to your chances of you setting out to pursue your dreams - or might it be so humiliating that you give up on it altogether? There are some who are driven to proving doubters wrong, but others might not respond so positively.

Going public with a plan to pursue an ambition means you also have to be ready to deal with the response of others should you fail. There's no shame in failure if you've tried your best, but it might still be something you'd prefer to manage on your own terms or just with people close to you.

'THERE IS NO RULE BOOK HERE. IT ALL COMES DOWN TO UNDERSTANDING YOURSELF, AND ASKING WHAT WILL SERVE YOU BEST WHEN IT COMES TO TAKING ON A NEW CHALLENGE.'

SUMMARY

We've come a long way in this first section, starting with understanding just what it takes to achieve something special and how that opportunity is available to us all. We've recognised that mindset and resilience are key in dealing with the ups and downs of what can be a long and testing journey, and discussed how to feel confident that we're facing the right challenge at the right time in our lives.

Next it's time to take a look at the best ways to work with others to achieve our goals. This doesn't just apply to football or other team sports. Even individuals who set out alone to make great things happen must rely on people they trust - sometimes with their lives - in order to reach the top of their game.

If we want to play well with others, that means bringing out a quality that we all possess. It's one that can help us to work as one in chasing our dreams, and be stronger for the experience - and that's kindness.

BE
KIND

What does it mean to be kind? Is it just about giving up your seat on the bus, or offering your last sweet to someone, or is there more to it than that?

The fact is there's so much more to kindness than good manners or being friendly or acting generously. It's about holding ourselves to a certain standard of conduct, and treating others as we hope that they will treat us. In a team, kindness is the glue that makes us stronger together. It means we're looking out for each other at all times. In a football or rugby squad, kindness between players can help allow everyone to perform to the best of their abilities both individually and collectively. Even when facing a personal challenge, kindness means we truly appreciate the efforts of those who support us, which brings us closer together. In a life boat crew or an army regiment, kindness can save lives.

Being kind is also about empathy. This is a word used to describe our ability to understand how other people are feeling. It's also about compassion, which is when we're drawn to help or support those who are going through a difficult time. Both empathy and compassion require us to be sensitive to those around us, but that doesn't make us soft. Being kind takes courage. It's about having the self-confidence to stand up for others and provide help when they need it so we can be greater than the sum of our parts. If anything, those who recognise the power that comes from this have the potential to be more resilient than most.

We are all capable of being mindful of others, even if we're on opposing sides or differ in our backgrounds or values. It really doesn't take much to be kind. In terms of where we're going in life, it's an aspect of our character that can take us places.

Ultimately, kindness benefits us as individuals as much as it does the people around us. It opens up opportunities, and the warm, calm and constructive outlook it enables can help us to successfully take on new challenges.

An Example to Everyone

As a youth player at Crystal Palace, I knew what was in store after a game if the team hadn't played well. Back in the changing rooms, the manager would be furious. Sometimes he'd spend up to an hour and a half yelling at us, which was common in that era of football. Nobody was allowed to leave until he'd finished. He'd go from one player to the next, shouting about how we'd disappointed him.

It was a difficult environment, and extremely challenging. The manager would get so worked up that he'd even throw balls around. Occasionally the odd teacup would hit the wall or crash to the floor! Most of us at Palace had faced rejection before, and we knew that the most effective way to get through the ordeal was by taking the criticism - no matter how harsh - and aiming to do better next time. We were a tough bunch but being the focus of that kind of shouting spree was never pleasant.

As a manager, I aim to follow a different approach. I played football in a time when the boss could work himself up into a rage in order to get a message across. Today, having experienced life as both a player and a coach, I try to get the best out of a team by taking a kinder approach: I calmly flag up what I like about a performance and then focus with complete honesty on areas that need improving. This helps me to effectively communicate with the players. It's also how I would like to be treated myself.

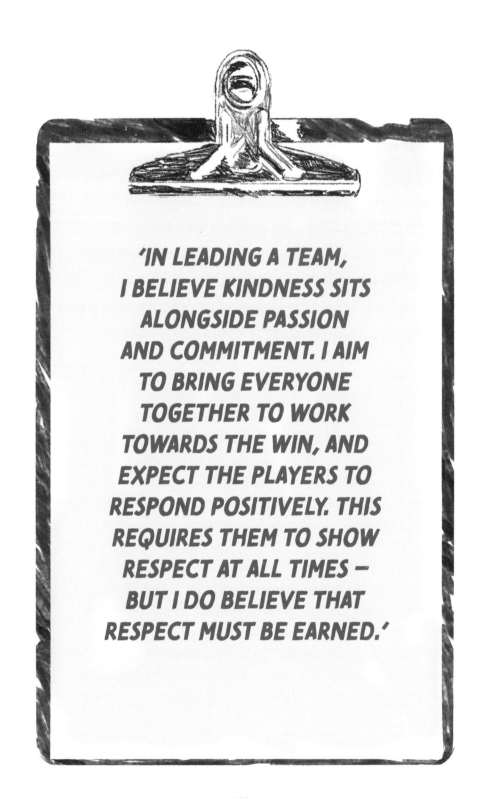

'IN LEADING A TEAM,
I BELIEVE KINDNESS SITS
ALONGSIDE PASSION
AND COMMITMENT. I AIM
TO BRING EVERYONE
TOGETHER TO WORK
TOWARDS THE WIN, AND
EXPECT THE PLAYERS TO
RESPOND POSITIVELY. THIS
REQUIRES THEM TO SHOW
RESPECT AT ALL TIMES –
BUT I DO BELIEVE THAT
RESPECT MUST BE EARNED.'

Respect Unwrapped

- 'Respect' is how we recognise that people, places or even objects represent important values.

- We can be respectful of a teacher, because they're helping us to learn; of places like churches and mosques; or of a work of art in a museum. We might respect a player who demonstrates good sportsmanship, or library rules that ask us to be quiet as others are reading.

- In some ways, respect helps us all to get along. Joining the end of a queue shows we recognise that the people already in line have been waiting longer than us - even though we don't know them. In the same way, dropping litter in a bin shows respect for our environment. It makes the world a better place for others as much as for ourselves.

- We don't have to agree with someone to respect them. A referee might show a yellow card to a player who disputes that they've done anything wrong, but the player still has to respect the decision. Why? Because both teams recognise that the ref upholds the rules of the game.

- In any friendship or relationship - personal or professional - respect brings people together. It inspires understanding and trust, as well as a feeling of security, and can help to create a positive environment in which to work, learn or play.

We've all faced people who expect us to look up to them simply because they're in a position of authority. In some way, they're demanding respect. The trouble is unless we recognise that they're worthy of that position, it's very hard for respect to come from the heart.

When respect is earned, however, it creates a strong bond. We don't have to be team captains or project leaders. Young or old, the fact is we are all capable of inspiring respect as much as we are of showing it, and that comes down to how we conduct ourselves.

Setting an example is about holding ourselves to account. It means being aware that our actions have consequences. Whether we're respectful towards others or grumpy and rude, it's always noted. It shapes people's opinions of us, and that can make a real difference to our lives.

If a tennis player spends more time throwing their racket around in a temper than returning balls, then it doesn't matter how talented they are, they might struggle to find anyone who wants to play against them. Should that same tennis player develop a reputation for being kind, considerate and polite, while also providing stiff competition across the net, their popularity can only rise.

What's more, it feels good to know we've made a positive impression on others. In effect, we've earned respect simply by being the best version of ourselves.

So, whatever situation we're in - as a player or a manager, or just as an individual who wants to make the most of life - setting a good example is a sure-fire way to make things happen for all the right reasons.

Six Simple Ways to Set an Example

Attitude is everything when it comes to making a great impression. It can also be surprisingly easy to upgrade your life so you can be your best self at all times:

1   **Be friendly.** Even small gestures like a warm smile or positive eye contact can strike the right note and set people at ease.

2   **Be engaged.** Connecting with people means putting them first, which doesn't take much. It's about tuning into how they're feeling as we speak, and showing an interest in them. Aim to put yourself in someone else's shoes, and see things from their perspective.

3   **Be considerate.** This is about showing respect towards other people, rules or conventions. It shows awareness, and people will rate you for that.

4   **Be polite.** Good manners go a long way with everyone. There's no need to be achingly formal all the time. Even just remembering to say 'please' and 'thank you' speaks volumes about your character.

5   **Be helpful.** Offering up your own time to help someone else with a task or a problem is a quality that can only invite respect. It shows generosity and a genuine kindness, and it feels good when people recognise that quality in you.

6   **Be a listener.** Even if you're in charge of a team, the only way to truly understand your players is with a listening ear. Creating the opportunity for people to voice their thoughts builds trust and invites respect.

Play Hard

Let's be clear, being kind or sensitive towards others doesn't mean we lack toughness. It's easy to think that someone with good manners and a positive attitude might lack that winning drive, but the reality couldn't be more different. If anything, all the qualities linked to being kind come from an inner confidence. They demonstrate that we're not afraid of what others think if we stop to offer help, or show respect for people or places instead of playing for laughs.

In my early years as a professional footballer, I had to adapt to environments and situations that demanded a thick skin. Every professional player has experienced a moment on the pitch where they've missed an opportunity and thousands of people in the stands have screamed at them. It's not pleasant, even if it's just a reflection of the passion supporters have for the team, and frankly the only way to get through it is to focus on playing well.

I had to find that mental toughness, otherwise I would have crumbled when I made mistakes. It wasn't always easy, but I still shook hands with the opposition at the final whistle and applauded the fans for their loyalty. The media could be equally challenging. After the match, I might find my performance pulled apart in the papers, or on radio or television. I had to learn not to take it personally, and recognise that the journalists had a job to do – just like I did.

Slowly, I learned to cope with these difficult moments. If anything, they improved my self-awareness. I knew I could be sensitive. In many ways, I saw it as a strength. That sensitivity meant I was open to the fact that I could always improve as a player, and this in turn meant I would focus on advice from the coaching staff. In short, I learned to deal with testing or even hostile environments while also remaining true to myself.

Dealing with any difficult situation demands a thick skin, but that doesn't mean we have to harden on the inside. It's about processing challenges rather than blocking them out, which means we can still hold ourselves to a high standard of conduct - no matter how testing things become.

If we can keep a level head while tempers flare around us, it shows that we are mentally stronger and more able to cope than those who have let their emotions get the better of them. At the very least, it earns respect, but it can also inspire others to behave in the same way.

Leading by Example

We don't always have to be in a position of power or authority to inspire respect in others. It can exist between friends, classmates and teammates, and helps everyone to get along and work well together. But how do we lead by example when we are tasked with bringing out the best in others?

When I was made captain at Crystal Palace, I didn't have any 'leadership' qualifications or credentials. Quite simply, I was considered to be one of the more sensible members of the team. But in those early years of my career, I picked up leadership skills through experience. Nobody sat me down and explained what was expected of me. It was just something I had to figure out for myself, mostly by having observed others in the role, and asking myself what I expected from a team captain.

When I moved to Aston Villa, a player called Andy Townsend wore the captain's armband. I was pretty much in competition with him for the same playing position on the pitch, and yet he did everything he could to make me feel welcome. Even if I was there to compete with Andy, his role as captain was to help me feel part of the team, and the fact he did so had a big impact on my own style of leadership going forward.

Working with teams today, we do talk to players about the qualities they might need to consider in preparing for leadership roles, but ultimately it will come down to learning on the job. I also find that, as we prove ourselves by our actions, then we're given yet more responsibility.

In my first few games as Palace captain, I certainly lacked a little confidence. Like facing any challenge, it was a question of stepping out of my comfort zone and finding my voice. When it comes to making ourselves heard, there is a temptation to raise the volume. Shouting might mean people hear us, and even take on board the message, but does it truly inspire respect?

In the dressing room as a youth player, braced for the boss to turn his displeasure on me, I'd never dared to turn the tongue-lashing into a conversation. Quite simply, the manager provided feedback that could often be summed up as 'We lost, you were rubbish, now get out of my sight!' – and we said nothing in response. Although the message that we had to improve was completely clear, the delivery left a lot of uncertainty about exactly how we should do it. We just had to work it out for ourselves, through trial and error.

This style of management works for some people, of course, and is in keeping with their personality. But, for me, I've found that leading with warmth enables me to communicate effectively with a team. If a player feels valued, and is given the sense that they belong, then ultimately that will be reflected in their performance. By communicating in this way, I hope to encourage them to develop the mental toughness they need to deal with difficult situations.

By taking a calmer approach to leadership, I find conversation and debate often come into the team talks. This is fine, and I welcome players challenging me to get the messaging right. In practice, it means if I announce that as part of our training we're going to climb over a ten-foot wall, then chances are most players will ask why. It's a fair question, of course, and so I'll explain that in order for everyone to complete the task successfully we'll be expected to work closely as a team. That means learning to cooperate and communicate, and trust one another not to let go when we need them the most!

In responding to the players' questions, I'll set out the reasons why we're taking on a task, and the skills it will help us to sharpen. As a result, with a clear objective in mind and a vision of what's possible if everyone works closely together, the team will be motivated.

I find this approach is more rewarding than just demanding they get on with it without daring to question me. It's about crediting everyone with the intelligence to recognise the benefits - to both the individual and the team - of undertaking a task, whether it's in training or during a game. My challenge as a manager is to communicate those benefits clearly.

Of course, as every player is different, some will follow instructions without question and others will seek to find their own way to deliver what's required. Whatever the case, my aim is to provide a vision of what we're striving to achieve, so the team can deliver results to the best of their abilities.

The First Eleven

Whether we're in charge of a team, or working on a project or a task with others who are in need of a little direction, leading by example can bring everyone together. And just as we need to understand ourselves before taking on a challenge, it's worth identifying our potential strengths as a leader as well as any areas in which we need to improve.

From the eleven leadership qualities below, select three you recognise in yourself and one that you'd like to shape up:

Positivity

Passion

Respectfulness

Integrity

Honesty

Humility

Approachability

Calmness

Openness

Clarity

Supportiveness

1.
....

2.
....

3.
....

....

and one you'd like to shape up

SUMMARY

Whatever we choose to do with our lives, our personal conduct is key. We can fight and scrap our way to the top, or follow a more rewarding path by playing fairly and to our strengths.

Earning respect in this way feels good. It doesn't take much to be kind and considerate towards others. This approach also helps to build the kind of constructive and supportive atmosphere that can allow us to focus on our goals.

We can be kind and tough at the same time, especially when life is difficult. In really challenging situations, for example, it helps to be able to listen as well as talk. Being on hand to offer help - as well as to accept when you need help yourself - can be the difference between giving up and pushing on for both yourself and for others. Quite simply, kindness can make us stronger - and by setting a good example, others will soon follow.

We all need leadership in life, whether we rely on others for guidance or we have to find it in ourselves. It often ends up being a blend of both, and this is one more reason why a positive outlook on life - and an awareness of the people around us - can bring out those qualities that help to guide and inspire. In a team, players might look to the captain, but when climbing a rock face solo it's down to the individual to find their inner leader.

We're talking here about human qualities like discipline, self-belief and focus. These qualities grow from experience but begin from being kind in our outlook on life. Kindness helps us to reach out and connect with others, which builds confidence and allows us to thrive. Ultimately, it's the springboard for greater things.

Stronger Together

We all rely on teamwork to make the most of life. From playing football, rehearsing as part of a band, or even doing the washing-up after someone else has cooked dinner, we have to cooperate to achieve a shared goal.

Sometimes, a team is clearly marked for all to see. When eleven footballers run out of the tunnel in matching kit, we know they're on the same side. But there's a whole host of members of that team that don't play on the pitch. I'm not just talking about the substitutes, the physios and the manager on the sidelines. Everyone from the coach driver to the club's canteen workers play an essential role. Without them, the players we know and love wouldn't make it to the game in the first place.

So, let's take time out to celebrate teamwork of every kind and in all walks of life. Whether we're pursuing an ambition on our own (but relying on a support crew) or we're part of a squad hoping to make it to the top, it's vital that we appreciate what makes a team tick. As individuals with kindness at heart, the more aware we can be of the connections between us the better we perform.

What Makes a Good Team?

A team is a group of people who work together to achieve a shared objective. In theory, every member knows the role they have to play, so that everyone gets along. At home, we could say our family is a team. At school, our class could be considered to be a team. From being a member of a department in the workplace to one of a group of friends casually shooting hoops on a basketball court, we all find ourselves in team situations where cooperation is key.

Cooperation Cracked

- When we cooperate with another individual or a group of people, it means we work together for the same purpose.

- Another word for cooperation is 'teamwork'.

- We may tackle the same task together - such as washing a car - or take on different roles with the same objective. Often, the latter approach allows us to play to our strengths. For example, if you're better at selling than cleaning, you might leave your friend with the bucket and sponge and go knock on the neighbours' doors to pitch your car-washing services.

- When it comes to effective teamwork, everyone needs to know what's expected of them at all times in order to achieve the goal.

- Teamwork always works best when there's clear communication.

In my time as a player and a manager, I have found the best football teams thrive on difference. If every member acts in the same way, then the team loses a certain spark. All players have unique personalities, of course, and bring their own qualities to the table. When a team works well, each player can play to their different strengths and create a formidable force.

A good team makes full use of these different personalities and qualities, and the role of a leader or manager is to shape a team into its best possible form. On the football pitch, for example, I might favour a goalkeeper and defence who are solid, dependable characters. Then, as I move forward through the formation, I'll start adding players who are more creative, or natural risk-takers who are quick to exploit an opportunity.

This helps to create a dynamic team made up of individuals with different qualities. It also means there's room for everybody.

Every Player Counts

Settling into a team can take time. We might know what we can offer, but how does that play out in a group situation? We need to get used to how the group works to find our place in it, which means understanding how our teammates perform together.

The first thing to recognise is that we won't all share the same qualities. Whether it's on a football pitch or the factory floor, everyone in a team has a place because they bring something different. What's more, it takes time - and effort and experience - to be good at what we do.

Sometimes it can feel like there's no place for us in a team. But there's always a position we can make our own, and in a way that involves working with others. We might not be the greatest surfer, for example, but we could be outstanding as a lifeguard. What's more, the respect we earn from all the people in the water makes us an essential player in that field. This is just one example of why our world is so rich and varied. If we all shared the same skills, it just wouldn't work at all. There'd be no progress or invention. Being passionate about different things also means there's space for us all to make a contribution to the best of our abilities – both as individuals and by working with others towards the same aim.

Stars behind the Scenes

It's often the case that behind every hero is a team that helped them to succeed. When Neil Armstrong landed on the moon, he did so thanks to an army of men and women across all manner of disciplines. But we often focus on that one famous individual in a spacesuit, without truly appreciating the staggering efforts that took place behind the scenes.

When it comes to our own ambitions, we can take comfort from this. We can't all be astronauts, but there's a whole host of opportunities available in the team supporting that bid. From rocket scientists to the cleaners at mission control, everyone involved plays an important role.

When Lewis Hamilton roars across the finish line to win another Formula One Grand Prix, he always comes on the radio to thank his team for their efforts. He's not just addressing the pit crew, but everyone at Mercedes – from the management to the receptionist at the front desk. I was lucky enough to spend a day at the Mercedes F1 headquarters, to observe and learn how a racing team performs under pressure.

During my visit, I was struck by the sight of a Mercedes Formula One car on display in the middle of the office building. It's there for members of all departments to admire - from aerodynamics to the press office - and serves to remind every single employee that despite their different skills, they share the same goal.

Small Role, Big Impact

Sometimes, when it comes to teamwork, we feel our contribution is so small that we don't make a difference. On the football pitch, a player might get just one or two touches of the ball during an entire match. But if those touches led to a shot on goal for a striker, or stalled an attack from the opposition, their contribution could be seen as vital.

A team is like an engine - it's made up of lots of complicated parts. Sometimes, it can be hard to see what role a single component plays in keeping the engine running, but we'd quickly find out if we removed it.

Understanding our role in a team is crucial when it comes to bringing out the best in us. Partly this comes down to experience, and figuring out our place in the team. It's also important to talk to everyone in that group, as well as those in charge - because the more we communicate, the clearer we can see how those moving parts work together.

Finding Our Feet

Joining a new team can be as exciting as it is challenging. Here is a chance to work with people who bring different skills to achieve the same goal, and yet first we have to understand how the organisation works and settle into the new group. Like the first day at school, it's hard to relax and be ourselves. At the same time, it's important that we find our place so we can perform at our peak.

When I'm new to a group, I find it's worth listening and observing to get a sense of how the team works. Often it's a case of figuring out the hierarchy – effectively, the social order of the group. Who is the loudest, the funniest, the most insightful or serious?

We might find ourselves drawn to people in the team who seem similar to us. That's okay. It's natural human behaviour to search for common ground, and it sometimes means that smaller groups can form within the team based on age or interests. In the England squad, for example, we have a group of players who love playing video games together. It's a great way for them to unwind off the pitch, while still remaining connected to the team. At the same time, I always encourage my players to get to know everyone in what is an inclusive team. By pushing themselves out of their social comfort zones, they can discover different viewpoints, forge new relationships and broaden their horizons. It benefits them as players, and strengthens the connections in the squad.

Team-Joining Tactics

If you're about to take your place in a new squad or group, here's how to settle in with kindness and confidence:

- Rather than trying to get to know everyone straight away, focus on one or two people who might share your interests.

- Kick off with a good question. Showing an interest in someone can be flattering. Their answer can also lead to more questions, and then the conversation starts flowing.

- Aim to be your best self. While it's tempting to fool around, gossip or laugh at other people's expense for attention, be aware that first impressions can be lasting.

- Your new friends might well introduce you to their friends in the group, and from there your social circle will begin to grow.

- If you can feel close to a few people in the team, and learn to get along with everyone else by being courteous and respectful, you'll soon feel like you belong.

Pick Me

In most team sports, joining the squad doesn't guarantee we'll play on every occasion. Usually, we join a pool of players. The coach then makes a selection depending on how they wish to shape the team that plays in the match.

So, once we've joined a squad, we need to make ourselves selectable. This begins by listening to the coach. There's no need to go sucking up to the person in charge - this might cause you to be disliked by everyone else. It's all about observing how the coach relates to the team. What are the behaviours that are praised, and which ones are frowned upon? In most cases, a manager will look for players who work hard, have a good attitude and generally put the team before themselves. At the same time, individual coaches will also look for a certain playing style, such as aggression or creativity. So, it's always worth asking what kind of team the coach is hoping to build, and what they're looking for in you.

In some ways, a player has to sense what the manager wants. Then they can set about working on delivering those qualities. The player's passion for the game is not in question here. Nor is their experience, if they've come this far and made it into the squad. But if they want to make themselves selectable, that player needs to show they completely understand what the manager wants from them. It's about being switched on to their role, and then delivering it to the best of their abilities.

This approach doesn't just apply to football, of course. In any team environment, we can only make a positive contribution by finding our place in the group first.

We Are United!

Since I was sixteen years old, I've played football with people from many different nationalities and religious or cultural backgrounds. During a match, nobody ever thinks in those terms. No matter how different we may be off the pitch, everyone is there for the same reason: to play well together, and hopefully win the game.

In many ways, this is the beauty of any sport. It celebrates the fact that, as human beings, we can unite for the sheer joy of playing the same game. Sport is a great equaliser, and also a brilliant ice-breaker.

Sometimes, players would join the team who didn't speak English as a first language. After a good training session or a match, it was always possible to share a joke or relive a moment using common words we all understood.

When we're younger, playing games is a brilliant way to break down barriers. During break times at school, I would happily join in a kickabout with older kids. Without a ball between us, chances are they would never have dreamed of speaking to me.

In any walk of life, teams bring people together. We can be different from each other in all sorts of ways, but when it comes to sharing the same objective, we work as one. This allows us to achieve things we might not be able to manage on our own. What's more, the shared experience of pulling together for a common aim can create friendships that last a lifetime.

Sometimes, teams from across different fields can cooperate to create something unique. Early in the Covid-19 pandemic, for example, engineers from the Mercedes Formula One team worked with University College London on developing a respiratory aid to help keep patients out of intensive care. Other big companies that worked together to design and produce ventilators for the NHS included Ford, Rolls-Royce and Siemens. They might all specialise in other fields, but they made great things happen by pooling their resources and sharing their knowledge and skills for the common good.

Ultimately, when it comes to working in teams - or even joining forces with another group to bring different skills into the mix - anything is possible.

The Christmas Truce

In December 1914, during World War One, a remarkable football match took place on the Western Front. British and German soldiers emerged from opposing trenches, laid down their weapons, and picked up a ball. It's believed the Germans won 3-2, but it wasn't the result that went down in history. It was the game itself, which briefly turned enemies into friends. In a sense, the two sides cooperated for a common goal: the chance to temporarily escape from the horrors of war, and celebrate Christmas and humanity.

SUMMARY

When we think about the most enjoyable moments in our lives, chances are we've experienced them alongside other people. There's something very special about working together towards a common goal. As a team - with family, friends, work colleagues or fellow players - there's real pleasure to be had from achieving something we couldn't necessarily do alone.

When England perform well, it's satisfying for me to watch the players celebrate. It makes all the hard work and effort to reach that moment worthwhile. I also know the staff members behind the scenes will be jumping for joy from the security to the reception staff. Above all, however, I can look out across the stadium and see the enjoyment we're bringing to the fans. I also know that joy will be shared by everyone watching on TV in homes and pubs across the country. That's when we're at our strongest as a team, and as a nation. It's a moment of happiness, when everyone comes together as one.

The Power of Positivity

Being kind is a positive force. It can show a desire to work with others to achieve great things together. When it comes to motivation - that drive to get something done - we draw our energy from all sorts of different places. Sometimes we crack on with a task because there'll be trouble if we don't, like a piece of homework we've put off until the last minute. It might not be the most enjoyable experience, but we're driven to tick it off the list and still learn something in the process.

Then there are the goals we pursue because we're passionate about them. Nobody has forced us to go on a journey like this, or makes us face up to the challenges along the way. We do it by choice because we love it, which means the energy that drives us has to come from the heart.

Both negative and positive drivers can help us to achieve great things. Often there's a mix of both in anything we do. We might not want to get up at dawn to go for a run, but if it's part of a training plan so we can be fit for a football tournament, then we'll head out as the sun peeks over the horizon.

Whatever goal is in our sights, it's always good to be aware of what's driving us. Generally, there's a positive reason for doing anything - even if it doesn't seem that way at the time - and so it's good to be able to remind ourselves of this when we need encouragement most. On any journey, there will be times when we question what we're doing. Perhaps we hit an obstacle with no easy way forward, or we're tired and feel ready to give up.

Then there are moments when it's tempting to take another path entirely. It can happen when chasing the goal is proving to be hard work, or even not very enjoyable. The trouble is, choosing that alternative path can come at a price if we're drawn to something that isn't necessarily in our best interests – or could even invite trouble. That's when the power of positive thinking can help remind us of our reasons for setting off on our journey in the first place, and the reward to be had from going the distance.

This doesn't mean we have to live our lives free of fun, or that we can't have relaxation time when we need it most. It's just about making informed decisions, rather than giving in to pressure from others and then wishing we'd done things differently.

The Driving Force

There is a question we should all ask ourselves before taking on a task. Sometimes we also need it as a reminder when things aren't going to plan. In short: What motivates us? What is the thing that keeps us pushing towards a goal no matter what? For me, the answer lies in the feeling of success and the enjoyment achieving something brings.

We can call this a positive driver, but there are also times when I set out to prove someone wrong. This is a negative driver, and it certainly played a role in my early career as a football player, when I was told I should think about becoming a travel agent instead. In some ways, a negative driver can create a burning desire to go out and show the doubters that we have what it takes to achieve our dream. Just be aware that when the journey becomes challenging, that negative reason can quickly fade in importance. On the other hand, a positive driver might see you through the toughest times, because that hunger to achieve comes from within. It doesn't guarantee success, but it does make it more likely to happen than if you'd set out fuelled by negativity alone.

Glass Half Full or Half Empty?

- This is an expression that doesn't just ask how you view the glass. It's a way of looking at life in general.

- People with a positive outlook tend to view the glass as half full. *There's still another half to enjoy!*

- Those who consider the glass to be half empty tend to be more negative in their outlook. *There's only half left . . .*

- People with a positive outlook are often called optimists. Those who opt for a negative view can be classed as pessimists. We are all individuals, of course, and many factors can affect our outlook at any time, but it's always good to be aware of the distinction.

When I think about my outlook, I believe that in general I am an optimist. Often, optimism combines with perseverance - which is a determination to succeed - when faced with setbacks. Whenever I have experienced tough times and searched inwardly for motivation, I tend to look for positives.

It's the same in my role as a manager. If I'm in charge of a team that hasn't performed well, or players have suffered injuries, I'll always look for that ray of hope. I'm not being optimistic for the sake of it, and I'm always realistic, but I like to focus on what might still be achievable. Why? Because dipping into negative thoughts is simply not constructive. When things haven't gone to plan, it stops us from considering what's still possible. As a way of thinking, it may protect us from further grief or disappointment, but it takes away the chance to prove to ourselves that we can succeed.

'BY LIMITING OUR AMBITIONS – FOR EXAMPLE, BY WRITING OFF OUR CHANCES OF WINNING AGAINST A STRONGER TEAM – WE'RE BASICALLY SETTING UP A BARRIER FOR OURSELVES. AND WITH SUCH A NEGATIVE MINDSET, IT'S VERY UNLIKELY WE'LL GO BEYOND IT.'

Make the Switch

It's never too late to switch a negative thought into a positive. Here's how to look at life in a more constructive light:

1 Recognise when a thought is negative or unhelpful: *I can't do this.*

2 Ask yourself why you think this way: *I've failed before.*

3 Aim to replace the thought with a positive: *I can try again.*

4 Practise until it becomes second nature: *I'll keep trying until I crack it.*

If we respond negatively to an obstacle or challenge, chances are we'll never overcome it. Thinking positively means we'll always find a way. With a little practice, what seemed impossible becomes an opportunity . . .

NEGATIVE	POSITIVE
I'll never succeed	Success is the result of hard work
I'm not good enough	I can pick up the skills I need
Mistakes mean failure	I can learn from the experience
It's too difficult	I can make it manageable
It's impossible	*Anything is possible*

It's rare to find anyone who is totally positive in everything they do. Whether we're losing games or flagging in a race - or asking if so much revision is really worthwhile - it's human nature to question if we're up to the challenges we set ourselves. The emotions that are stirred up can sometimes make us feel hopeless. What matters is how we respond to them.

It's only natural to express our disappointment if things haven't gone to plan. What we do after that – if we learn to add positivity to our outlook – can make the difference between giving up and pushing on.

Another great thing about positivity is that it can influence the people around us. It's an energy that helps others focus on their goals when times are tough, and can even bring a team together.

Some people, whether or not they're leaders, possess a personality that can inspire and drive a group in the right direction. They might train well, or generally set a good example. Then there are those with a negative outlook, who don't respond constructively to challenges. Finally, there's a group in the middle, to which most of us tend to belong. We can choose to adopt a negative attitude – like dwelling on losing a match – or focus on the positive group, who are busy working out what they can learn from the experience in order to improve for the next game.

The power of positivity could be seen during the football matches played with social distancing restrictions to combat Covid-19. With games staged in empty stadiums, it struck me that some players missed the energy that can come from the crowd. That energy isn't always positive, of course, but even the experience of having thousands of people groaning at you over a missed pass can be a driving force to do better.

Ultimately, whether we pursue an ambition by ourselves or in a group, we are never truly alone. What's more, everyone on our journey – whether they're on the pitch or behind the scenes – provides an energy we can call upon to help us progress. The key is in how we respond to this energy. If we do so positively, and in a spirit of kindness, I believe we are more likely to achieve success.

Facing Our Fears

Over the last ten years, every coaching course I've been on has involved taking a personality test. I've got a whole collection of the results now, and they aim to help me know myself better. As well as flagging up my strengths, the results of these tests have helped me to accept that I'm just not very good at certain things. Being naturally quite introverted, for example, my instinct is to shy away from the spotlight.

It's perfectly normal to be weaker in some things than others. We're only human, after all. What matters is how we face up to these shortcomings. The first step is to recognise our weak points. Then we can accept them as something to work on, before figuring out how we can do better.

It's very easy to get worked up about our weaknesses. Having them is frustrating, and we can feel like we've let ourselves down - as well as other people. The trouble is that approach does nothing to help us deal with them.

When I'm working with others, I find it helps if I can turn my weaknesses into something we can laugh about. So, rather than being embarrassed about the things I'm not so good at, I smile about them instead. It takes away any awkwardness and fear, and even helps me to think they're something I can overcome. As a result, rather than feeling like I should stay within my limits as an introvert, I'm able to leave my comfort zone and step up.

No matter what the outcome, it all begins with finding the courage to face a reluctance or fear. It doesn't necessarily mean we'll go on to turn that weakness into a major strength, but we can at least learn to be comfortable with it.

We are not alone in having weaknesses. No one can be good at all things, and it helps to recognise this in others as much as ourselves. As a manager, part of my job is identifying whether it's more effective to focus on a player's weaker abilities or work around them. For example, there might be a great striker who doesn't shine at tackling. There's always room for improvement, of course, even if it's just raising awareness with them. Then again, that striker might not have the physical build to become an exceptional tackler. In that case, rather than spending ages addressing their tackling, it's better to focus on their flair for shots on goal. This way, we can work together to make them truly great at their strength: goalscoring.

In a similar way, there are always people who like to have their day mapped out before it begins. This rigid approach might seem like a weakness, but frankly it's just how they're wired and that's fine. Often individuals like this can be analytical thinkers, and they are key components among the range of personalities in any strong team. It simply means that, as a manager, I have to think carefully before suddenly changing the time of a training session, and make sure I provide plenty of notice. That way, I won't throw anyone out of sorts, and they can focus on performing to the best of their abilities.

We can all raise our game when it comes to addressing a fear, weakness or any aspect of our personality where we struggle to be flexible. And it begins by acknowledging how our weakness restricts us or impacts the team. By facing up to it, suddenly we can view it as something to work around - or even overcome.

Ditch the Duvet Day

On waking up, we've all experienced that feeling that something didn't go well the day before. Whether it was a bad day at school or on the football pitch, the temptation is to relive it in our minds, groan to ourselves and pull the duvet back over our heads.

Here's how to see those moments in a different light, and prevent a negative outlook from setting in:

- **Be honest.** It takes courage to come to terms with setbacks and admit we've made mistakes or done something wrong.

- **Accept what's happened.** We can't change the past, but we can take responsibility. Owning our actions is a brave move, and can only invite respect.

- **Find the positive.** From learning a lesson to pledging to improve, something good can come from every situation.

- **Face the world.** Get up, get dressed and get set to make a difference to the day. It's a vital first step towards moving on from what's happened and feeling stronger for the experience.

- **These are the days that build us.** It's only by getting through the tough times that we recognise that there is always a way. That, in a nutshell, is what positivity is all about.

Stay Strong

Going after a goal of any kind demands focus. We have to keep our goals in sight through the good times and the bad, and also in the face of distraction. That can be tough when there are lots of other things going on that seem like fun. It's all about balance, of course, and fun should play an important part in all of our lives. There's room for it while pursuing any challenge, in fact. It only becomes a problem when we seek a good time as an escape from necessary hard work, or get involved in something that could cost us success.

I never really got into trouble at school, for one simple reason: I was scared of being told off. I can't say I was always good, but there was definitely a fear that kept me in check. I also knew that if I got on the wrong side of my teachers then my dad would hold me responsible. As it turned out, this was a useful way of thinking. Later as a youth player, when I didn't get picked at county trials, I looked to myself for a reason rather than blaming the coach.

When I failed to get selected, I knew that I had to improve. That meant making sure that my social life didn't get in the way of my football. In many ways, this taught me the value of personal responsibility.

It helped that I was on the shy side. I didn't really feel comfortable at parties, and I was aware that hanging out with certain people could possibly lead to trouble down the line. It didn't stop me from being friendly with them; there just came a point when I would head off for training or a match, and they would do their own thing - and that worked for everyone.

In groups, it can be hard to be an independent thinker. When everyone else is set on doing one thing, the easiest thing is to follow. It takes courage to opt out or head in a different direction. I've been on teams with players who tended not to get involved in group activities outside training. At the time they could be viewed slightly negatively by the rest of the players (myself included), but now I have respect for them. It meant they were comfortable with themselves and knew what they wanted from life. They were just as committed to the team as everyone else, and were on good terms with everyone. They just didn't feel the need to join the others off the pitch in activities that might have been frowned on by the club. Why? Because being the best they could be at football mattered to them more than anything else.

No matter what goal lies at the end of our journey, everything comes back to the reason why we set off in the first place. It doesn't necessarily have to be some incredible dream - it can just be the thought of a life we can take pride in that's free from trouble. If we can remind ourselves of this at all times, and especially when things are tough, then we can stay on course and still have fun.

Sure-Fire Ways to Stay on Track

- **Understand yourself and your goals.** Knowing what makes you a decent person helps to build self-confidence. It will also give you a sense of independence that enables you to make informed decisions rather than just following the crowd.

- **Consider the consequences of your actions.** If it's going to have a negative impact on others, ask yourself if that's how you'd like to be treated.

- **Take pride in your conduct.** You don't have to be the best-behaved, but people respect those who consider others and have a sense of right and wrong.

- **Overcome obstacles.** Even if you're in trouble, or feel things are heading that way, with focus and determination there is always a way to move on from it with valuable lessons learned.

- **Help is always out there.** It's just a question of admitting to yourself that things aren't right and reaching out. It takes courage, but earns respect.

SUMMARY

A positive outlook on life can inform everything we do. Optimism doesn't have to be our defining quality, but it can help us to view life as an exciting challenge rather than a failure in waiting.

At the same time, positivity isn't something we can all suddenly switch on like a light. If we've fallen into the habit of negative thinking, then it's hard to see the glass as anything other than half empty. But we still have the potential to change our lives for the better.

So, rather than aiming for an instant transformation in the way you look at the world, begin with small steps. Consider a task or challenge in your life. It doesn't have to be much - even just making the bed in the morning. This time, rather than viewing it as a chore, focus on how it feels to complete it. It should feel good to know you've made the effort to raise your standards by a notch. It's only one minor alteration in attitude, and it's hardly going to be the crowning moment of your day, but if you take the same positive approach to every task then it can lead to a major upgrade in outlook over time.

Change has to start somewhere, and we each have the power to begin that process. It starts with an awareness of the way we view life, and reminding ourselves that a positive outlook brings opportunities that we might otherwise miss. It doesn't guarantee success, of course, but when we encounter those setbacks that might have once persuaded us to give in, then we get up . . . and we go again.

Dare
to
Try

When someone shines at a particular task - from kicking a football to sketching a portrait - people often say they're a natural. This can be flattering for that person to hear, but it can leave everyone else feeling like they're not good enough.

The fact is we all begin with the same potential to do great things with our lives. In certain fields like sport there may be physical advantages to being built a certain way - but when it comes to skills, we're talking about things that can be learned. This is true for everyone, and we all have to start from scratch. That kid doing great things with the ball? The artist sketching a portrait everyone else admires? Chances are they've just been practising their skills for some time, and enjoy what they do. And even though they've already started their journey and become really good, there will always be room for them to learn and improve.

With the right mindset and a positive outlook, anyone can follow in their footsteps. The fact is we can all get better at anything we choose to do. We might not do it to a world-class standard, but that's fine. What matters is that we enjoy the process as we try to perform to the best of our abilities, and feel rewarded by the outcome. But in order to make it that far, we have to prepare for what lies ahead. Quite simply, before we can become good at something, we must recognise that there will be challenging moments that will tempt us to give up.

Whether we're facing a task that seems impossible to conquer or we feel like the commitment involved in chasing our dream is all too much, thoughts will come into our mind that are from our 'inner critic'. This is the subconscious voice that casts doubt on our ability to achieve things, undermines our confidence, and effectively suggests that our time would be better spent watching TV on the sofa.

When our inner critic speaks, we can choose to go in one of two directions. We can give up as instructed, or we can find ways to improve in order to crack on and demonstrate that anything is possible.

When I first became the football manager at Middlesbrough, the experience didn't immediately match my expectations. I'd just retired as a player (and captain) at the end of the previous season, and I kicked off the next in my new role. I was excited by this development in my career, but it all happened very quickly. Looking back, there just wasn't much time for me to stop, think and properly prepare. Everything was new to me, and with so many demands from everyone around me I didn't feel like I was truly getting a grip on things.

This is when my inner critic kicked in. Because I felt like I wasn't in full control of the situation, I began to ask myself if I was even cut out for the role. I had read that in his time in charge of Manchester United, the legendary Sir Alex Ferguson would be at the training ground from eight o'clock every morning. Naturally, I felt I had to do the same thing. What I didn't realise was that he left early to deal with all the other issues his job demanded, whereas I would be the last to leave and simply ran out of time for everything else. So I'd stay up late to deal with paperwork, rushing through meals and not getting enough sleep.

Unlike me, Sir Alex had learned how to organise his time and energy. He'd worked out that an early start with the squad at the training grounds would get his day into a good rhythm. But as I struggled to get on top of things – feeling increasingly tired and run down – the critic in my head became harder to ignore. How could I manage a team, I thought to myself, if I was struggling to manage myself?

All I knew was that I had learned to conquer challenging situations before. If I was going to improve in my new job, then I needed to control my inner critic. It was leading me towards focusing on the negatives at a time when I needed to act constructively. So I reminded myself that everyone has to start somewhere, which we all need to remember when it comes to learning how to get better at something.

Hands Up!

There comes a time, often early in our education, when we shoot up our hand to answer a question, get it wrong and then think perhaps we won't be in such a hurry again. It's human nature, especially in a group environment. Nobody wants to be the centre of attention for making a mistake. As a result, it's easy to fall into the habit of feeling like we know the answer but avoiding the gaze of the teacher in the hope that they'll pick on someone else.

But while it might keep the attention away from us, does that really help us learn?

The fact is if we want to get good at anything, whether it's a subject at school or a sport of any kind, we have to dare to try. And that means overcoming the inner critic that tells us to hold back. In a sense, that negative inner voice is really just the mind's way of trying to protect us from feeling awkward or embarrassed. *We've been in this situation before,* it says as it sounds the alarm. As a result, we stay in our comfort zone, as if bad things might happen if we step beyond it.

Not putting our hand up doesn't just happen in the classroom but in any group situation. When I address a team of professional footballers and ask them a question, I expect almost everyone to stare at the floor. So my strategy in that situation is to ask a player directly instead, and be sure to treat their response with respect. Why? Because whether or not it's the right answer, the act of engaging and having a go is a learning experience. Often I'm just after an opinion, and so there's no incorrect answer. It's more a springboard for conversation and debate. Every response has value - and as other players begin to speak up, those inner critics that have been holding them back are silenced.

Raising our hands to answer a question is a simple act of learning, but it takes courage. All too often we give in to our anxiety about getting it wrong, and stay quiet. Ultimately, if we want to be successful in pursuing our ambitions, we have to overcome this most basic of obstacles. And that doesn't just mean answering questions, but also asking for help when we need it.

Experience will show that there's nothing to fear in speaking up. Nobody is going to point and laugh, which is something we often instinctively imagine. If anything, putting up our hand or stepping forward into a situation is an act of engagement that inspires respect. Also, the more we get involved – and recognise there's nothing to worry about – the easier it becomes.

'PRACTICE REALLY DOES MAKE PERFECT, EVEN IF WE DON'T GET THE ANSWER RIGHT FIRST TIME.'

How to Ask for Help

If you're feeling left behind, don't watch everyone fade into the distance. Here's how to get the support you need in order to catch up:

- **What's the problem?** Be honest with yourself about where you need help. Is it a single issue, or a general area? Make notes if it helps, so you can communicate clearly.

- **Identify who can help.** It might be a teacher, a coach, or maybe someone further ahead of you on the same journey. Find someone you trust and use them as a lifeline.

- **Pick a good time.** Asking someone for help in the middle of a lesson or training session might mean they can't give you the attention you need. Instead, flag up that you'd like to talk at a convenient time.

- **Be clear.** Explain the problem, and then be ready to listen.

- **Be constructive.** People will want to help you. What matters is that you can offer a positive attitude and a willingness to learn. This way, you can establish a useful and effective plan together and then stick to it.

- **Review the situation.** Arrange a date to check in again, to be sure you're back on track - even if you need more help in getting there.

How to Shine

All sorts of factors feed into the desire to reach the top of our game. From the footballer who dreams of representing their country to the pupil who wants to become a doctor one day, our goals are shaped by lots of reasons.

No matter what we choose to do, if we want to shine then it helps to feel valued.

It's easy to look at stars in sport and the creative arts, and measure their success in terms of trophies and awards or by the size of their social media following. The same goes for people who have studied hard to earn qualifications and letters after their names, like scientists and lawyers, but not all of us will have such visible achievements for our efforts. Many roles or challenges can be just as demanding as those that are celebrated or recognised, which can leave some feeling sidelined. In this situation, it can be hard to feel like we're making progress or achieving true success.

In recent times, living with measures to control Covid-19, our understanding of what makes a hero has been shaken up dramatically. As a national football team, which includes top-class players idolised across the world, we found ourselves effectively without a role. We were of no importance, and frankly no use! Until football came back – and played in empty stadiums – we stayed at home like everyone else and recognised the true worth of those who kept the world turning: the key workers.

We're talking about everyone from delivery drivers and nursery teachers to bin men and women, supermarket and postal workers – and, of course, our incredible NHS staff. Every single one had a critical part to play, and almost overnight we as a nation came to fully value their importance.

As we get through the pandemic, I hope this newfound respect for key workers continues. Not only does this appreciation show that we all have a part to play in our society, it's an opportunity for workers who perhaps felt overlooked in the past to feel valued. Their work is critical, and not just during these extraordinary times, and this knowledge should be a source of pride to them. They've had a positive effect on us all, which must be a good feeling. And for many, that might be what motivates them to become truly exceptional at what they do.

That drive to progress and shine in a role, goal or ambition is available to everyone, of course. It's down to us as individuals to seize it, and then work at becoming the best version of ourselves.

Get Better

Having taken on the role of manager at Middlesbrough, it was only natural that I wanted to do the job to the best of my abilities. But I recognised the challenges straight away, because it all seemed so unfamiliar to me. From my experience as team captain I knew how to talk to players, but there was so much more to my new role. From player selection and team strategy to communicating with the board and the media, altogether it seemed quite overwhelming.

With my inner critic's voice rising in volume, I set about establishing a way forward.

Before we can get better at any task or skill, we have to learn how to do it. Think about riding a bike. We need stabilisers for some time while we build up the experience and skill needed to wobble off on two wheels. From there, improvement comes from time spent in the saddle.

Practice really is key in almost everything we do. There's no substitute for learning as we go along - often under the watchful eye of a trainer or expert, though this isn't always possible. A surgeon can't afford to go wrong, which is why it takes years of practical study to qualify in medicine. In a very different way, a football manager won't last long in the job if their team fails to win matches. The roles might be a world apart, but in both cases success is the only acceptable outcome. In any challenge like it, that means finding a way to progress with confidence and positivity.

With no school for managers available to me, I had to rely on two key qualities in order to silence my inner critic, tackle the job and improve: the belief that I could get better, and a vision of where I wanted to be. Both relied on a positive outlook, as well as previous experience in other areas of my career. I had suffered setbacks as a footballer, after all, and had found a way to toughen up in order to overcome them.

Away from football, I had also embraced skills that didn't come naturally to me, like public speaking. When I think about where I first picked up some experience in finding my voice, I go back to my time at school, when I braved putting up my hand to answer questions.

Like everyone, I'd had to learn to get over my reluctance to be the one who answers incorrectly. Over time, as experience taught me there was no shame in having a go, the worry about getting it wrong just faded. I became used to speaking up, which helped in my career when invitations arrived for me to give talks at conferences and dinners. Facing five hundred people is very different from answering a question in class, of course, but that early experience had taught me to take a breath and speak up. It was a foundation for me to build on, and a first step towards getting better at a skill.

Not every skill begins with putting up our hand in class, but almost every experience that involves stepping out of our comfort zone can prove useful. It all comes down to finding the courage to try, followed by the self-belief and commitment to build on those skills.

Today, I've learned to be comfortable with public speaking – something that didn't come naturally to me – just because I've done so much of it. Sometimes it goes well, but there are often occasions when I feel it could have been better. I can still feel nervous beforehand as well, but I've learned to project confidence. At the same time, I think a little nervousness can be useful. It gets the blood pumping, and helps us to focus on the task ahead. It means we can complete it knowing we gave it our best shot. That has to be better than being so completely relaxed that we take our eye off the ball or make foolish mistakes.

In learning how to deliver my best as a football manager, a post I went on to hold for three years at Middlesbrough, the process was the same. I had set out to become a footballer, not a team boss, and so this was an opportunity to learn new skills. I was prepared to try, and had plenty of experience in stepping out of my comfort zone. I just needed to remind myself of the one thing that would help me to feel comfortable in the role, so I could focus on delivering my best efforts.

We're talking about self-confidence here, or self-esteem – terms that can be used to describe how positively we view ourselves and our abilities. Some people might feel they've never really had much self-esteem, and others can suffer a drop in self-confidence during a challenging episode in life. The good news is self-confidence is something we can develop, rebuild and grow – and sometimes we need only remind ourselves that we're more capable than we believe. Whatever goal or ambition we have in mind, having that all-important belief in our abilities and potential will keep us moving forward.

In our comfort zones, it is easy to feel comfortable in our own skin. With self-confidence, we can still feel sure about ourselves and our purpose once we step into the unknown.

Kick-Start Your Confidence

Being comfortable with who we are can help build the confidence needed to embrace new experiences and build skills. Here's how:

- **Kick comparisons into touch.** It's easy to look at people who have mastered a task or skill and feel we'll never measure up. Aim to focus on yourself here, and consider those ahead of you on the journey to be a source of inspiration - or even help.

- **Get involved.** Holding back from trying any task or activity can just reinforce fears that we'll never be good enough. Everyone has to start somewhere, after all.

- **Find a friend.** Storing up worries can quickly see them grow. It can also distort how you feel about yourself. Having someone you trust who you can talk to at any time will help to put things in perspective.

- **Identify your strengths.** It doesn't have to be much. A broad smile or a sense of humour can earn a positive response and leave you feeling good. The next step is to build on it. As you start to shine, so your confidence will grow.

SUMMARY

We all have an inner critic, but with confidence it's possible to replace that critic with a motivating force we can call an inner coach. When we're midway up a mountain climb, and the peak seems a long way off, we need to be able to summon that positive spirit. It's a way of thinking, as well as viewing challenges, that can inspire us to stay focused on our goals.

Sometimes just leaving our comfort zone demands the same mental push. Whether we're putting up our hand in class or parachuting out of a plane, we have to believe in ourselves first. We rely on this same quality when it comes to demanding physical activities. Playing ninety minutes of football or hoping to achieve a PB at a Parkrun is going to involve some physical suffering, but then it's impossible to achieve anything in life without encountering a little pain. If we have the self-confidence to know that we'll get through it, we have every chance of getting better at whatever we choose to pursue.

No matter how grand our ambitions, if we just dare to try then we really can become fearless.

Keep Calm, Stay Focused

We've seen that kindness can be a strength. It gives rise to all manner of qualities such as positivity, compassion and empathy, which can help us to play and work together to the best of our abilities.

We can all be kind. It's a gift within us all that can change lives. Combined with the boldness required to believe that anything is possible, kindness can equip us to prepare for new challenges without ever feeling held back. We can live by example, holding ourselves to a standard of conduct that inspires respect, admiration and support in anything we choose to do.

In some ways, we've been talking about an inner journey so far. Having learned to understand ourselves - and placing kindness at the heart of everything we do - let's prepare for the practical steps involved in taking on any challenge or ambition. For the student about to sit down to begin revising for exams, the apprentice ahead of their first day at work or the young filmmaker with a vision, this is the moment before a journey that could change lives. It's just a question of keeping calm, staying focused and taking one step at a time.

The Power of Fun

During England's 2018 World Cup campaign in Russia, we had very few days between matches. Everyone had worked incredibly hard in the build-up to the tournament, and the team knew that they needed to perform to the very best of their abilities. But it wasn't just about the physical test of playing matches at an international level, and the strain that can put on the body. Mentally, the national squad carried the hopes and dreams of the whole nation.

The players were cooped up in a hotel complex, under pressure in all sorts of ways, and we needed to make the most of the short amount of recovery time between fixtures. So, we sent the lads into the swimming pool, and threw in a bunch of inflatable unicorns.

In any sport, pool sessions can aid physical recovery. This is down to the fact that water provides gentle resistance to help ease tired muscles and reduce soreness. But they can also be quite boring. So, in order to create an environment where the players weren't focused on getting out of the water as soon as possible, we introduced an element of fun. Instead of the squad going through the motions in the pool, they clambered on board the inflatables, laughed and larked about.

As a result, the players enjoyed an effective recovery session that didn't just benefit their bodies, but also their minds. It was a chance to escape from the pressures of the tournament, and showed that fun can play a central role in any challenge.

In every organisation I have visited, I find that people are most effective in their jobs if they're able to enjoy themselves. If it's just work, they don't perform to the best of their abilities. There is a balance to be had, of course. In the England training camps, it can't be a laugh all the time. When we're working, we are focused, but there has to be space for everyone to enjoy themselves as well.

Take the Challenge

In the military, officers talk about finding humour in adversity. Their world can be incredibly serious, and sometimes even deadly. As a result, they consider a moment of laughter to be vital. Ultimately, it lifts the spirits and keeps the troops focused on their tasks and challenges.

Before the 2018 World Cup, the England squad had an opportunity to spend a few days with the Royal Marines at a training camp. I wanted to take the players out of their comfort zones and into a world that was unfamiliar to them, and see how they responded. At the same time, it had to be enjoyable and act as a team-building exercise, and so we brought all the support staff with us as well.

To my surprise, I discovered a lot of players had never camped out before, or cooked for themselves outdoors. It was completely new to them, but everyone enjoyed the experience. And it helped to create the right atmosphere for the real work, when we focused on how the marines worked together under the kind of pressure that could have deadly consequences in the field of battle.

On the football pitch, if we get things wrong we're disappointed, but for soldiers the stakes are far higher. We looked at the level of detail they put into their work to make sure everything goes to plan. Then, putting the lessons we'd learned into practice, the whole squad - including me - were tasked with helping each other over a tough assault course. Cooperation was essential, and it was fascinating to watch some of the younger players - who had fitness on their side - help the older staff members through underwater pipes and over climbing walls.

Throughout that exercise, in which everyone was treated as an equal, I witnessed trust and respect grow across our group. The staff were grateful to the players for their help, and the players rated the older guys for giving it their best shot. It was a learning experience all around and incredibly tough work, but we had fun and we left the camp feeling rewarded on so many levels.

England's experience with the Royal Marines is just one example of how we aim to strengthen team spirit in a short space of time. With players coming together from several different clubs, we often don't have long to prepare and form the bonds required to perform at an international level. We're also a young squad, and so presenting new challenges can help everyone grow and better understand each other. By taking on an unfamiliar task that demanded close teamwork, we achieved our goal of working hard and having fun.

How to Enjoy the Journey

Some say that if you love what you do then you never have to work again. There's a great deal of truth in this. It can even apply to a task like exams, if you can focus on the fact that it'll open up the chance to pursue a dream opportunity. There's always going to be moments on our journey that we enjoy more than others, but here's how to make the most of it all:

- **Be passionate.** Chasing an ambition or a goal with your heart and soul will always make the journey more enjoyable. Why? Quite simply because you want to be there.

- **Make friends.** Stepping out of your comfort zone often brings you into contact with new people. Some will be on the same path as you, which immediately gives you something in common.

- **Take time out.** By being bold and kind in your outlook, chances are you'll be motivated to work hard. Just make sure you build time into your schedule to rest and recover. It's not just good for the body if your challenge is physically demanding. In anything we do, it's vital that we take care of our mental welfare as well, and find ways to relax.

- **Learn to laugh.** Even if your ambition is no laughing matter, there's always time for humour. If you can laugh at yourself, or share a joke with others, it can put tough times in perspective. Just be sure not to laugh at the expense of others - by being kind at all times - and you'll find those lighter moments can be a bonding experience.

- **Be creative.** This doesn't just apply to your free time, but anything from training to a revision session. Fun is a brilliant motivator, and can help you to focus on goals when it feels like you're making an effort for little reward. In short, hard work doesn't have to feel like a long haul.

Raising Our Game

We've learned that having fun and playing hard can help us in our preparations. Whether we're training, rehearsing or getting ready for any other task or challenge, these are important components that rely on being bold in vision and kind at heart.

'FOR MANY PEOPLE, THE IDEA THAT HARD WORK CAN BE FUN IS SOMETHING THEY HAVE TO LEARN FROM EXPERIENCE, BUT ONCE THEY DO THERE IS NO TURNING BACK.'

Now let's look at how small changes in our everyday lives can go a long way to helping us achieve big dreams. We're talking about raising our personal game here. In terms of self-discipline, these are adjustments to our behaviour that might well have to be practised. Once the benefits become clear, however, they quickly become second nature . . .

Set the alarm

- One of the simplest ways to make the most of each day is to create a routine. However you fill your time, aim to begin by waking up at the same time each morning.

- It might hurt waking up to the alarm the first few times, but by getting into the habit, your body clock will take over to some degree. The more often you wake up at the same time - along with practising a regular bedtime routine - the easier it becomes.

- Once you're awake, get up, get dressed and seize the day! I like to exercise first thing in the morning. It means I can be finished before the demands of my schedule begin.

- Setting the alarm helps to create structure to each day. It means you can make plans with time to deliver on everything, before heading to bed feeling tired and fulfilled.

Greet people

- Good habits have a huge impact. We all know first impressions count, so why not create one from the moment you meet someone?

- Rather than stare at your phone or your feet, locked in your own little world, reach out to the people around you with a nod and a greeting.

- Anyone who volunteers to say 'hello' or 'good morning' goes up in my estimation. Whether or not I know them, the effort is always noted. It's a small gesture that is crammed with good values: respect, politeness and positivity.

- We have quite a culture within the England team of making sure we greet each other in this way. If we're staying in a hotel or a training camp, we make a point of acknowledging each other, and the bond this helps build speaks volumes.

- Frankly, greeting people feels good. You make eye contact and smile, and when that person responds in kind it's a buzz that's hard to beat.

'... and how are you?'

- If you've found the courage to greet someone, why not take things to the next level and follow it up?

- Asking after someone shows you're genuinely interested in them. It's flattering and likely to invite a positive response.

- It can also kick-start a conversation, which can lead to all manner of opportunities.

- These are personal skills and qualities that people remember. Basic manners cost nothing, but can prove invaluable over time – especially once they become second nature.

We all respond to advice in different ways. Some people will think about setting their alarm, and then skip it in favour of a lie-in. Others might consider greeting someone, only to lose their nerve because it feels new and weird. All I can suggest is that you stick with it. Play around with the suggestions so they suit you. Experiment until it all falls into place. We're not talking about a massive transformation here – just a little commitment to encourage self-discipline and a positive attitude. Why? Because when it comes to taking on any new task or challenge, these are winning qualities. They'll help to bring a sense of calmness that feels good and allows you to focus on the task at hand. Just give it a shot for a week at first, and then another week . . . and as that becomes a natural routine just see what a difference it makes to your life.

Concentrate on Controllables

In order to perform to the best of our abilities, we have to stay focused and calm. From preparing to take a penalty kick, recording a podcast or speaking in assembly, if we approach any task in a spin it could undo all the hard work that's gone before it.

Some pursuits demand absolute calm and focus because safety is an issue. Awaiting the green light on the grid, a Formula One racing driver can't afford to let nerves get the better of them. They're about to power towards the first turn at high speed, going wheel to wheel with their rivals. With so much going on and so rapidly, how do they stop themselves from being overwhelmed?

The answer is in their minds. It's about making the choice to concentrate only on those elements of the task that they can control.

The racing driver can't know who might get a better start than them, just as a student facing an exam can't have any certainty that their preferred question will be included in the paper. Thinking otherwise is wasted energy – a distraction – and just likely to stoke up stress. But it's human nature to let our thoughts get carried away under pressure, and it takes time and experience to learn how to master them.

Under Control

Imagine yourself in these situations and consider what is in your power to influence. You'll be surprised by how much you can cut out from your mind:

TASK
PLAYING FOOTBALL

What can I control?

My abilities

Team tactics

The opposition

The crowd

The referee

The weather

The result

TASK
BAKING COOKIES FOR FRIENDS

TASK
CATCHING THE SCHOOL BUS

What can I control?

(The recipe)

(The ingredients)

(The cooking process)

The verdict on my cookies

What can I control?

(My time-keeping)

The bus arriving on schedule

Whatever goal or task you're facing, the more you practise working only with controllables, the easier the task becomes. Chances are you'll find yourself approaching any challenge - from the routine to the extraordinary - with a sense of calm you didn't possess before.

Concentrating on controllables can help us to manage our thoughts under pressure. It can also encourage us not to look too far ahead during those times when we need to feel especially positive and confident. Looking ahead is easily done when we're faced with a challenge containing many variables, and doubts can quickly set in. One moment we're preparing to climb the rock face, the next we're imagining ourselves stuck near the top with the rescue chopper swooping in to save us. Rather than focus on the fact that we're equipped and trained, with full safety measures in place, our thoughts skip beyond the steady climbing process to an outcome beyond our control.

This is called catastrophising. It's triggered when our anxieties encourage us to dwell on the worst-case scenario.

As a young manager, I worried about getting the sack. It's one of those jobs in football that can quickly come to an end if the team fails to perform. People would tell me I was always just three matches away from losing my job, and that piled on the pressure. I began to dwell on the fact that I would be seen as a failure – and that it would affect my future somehow.

Then I registered the fact that I was basically catastrophising – dwelling on worst-case scenarios that had yet to happen and were beyond my control – and I set out to get a grip.

I had let my brain go on a journey, and I needed to reel it in. I began by asking myself what I could control, and how I could influence those outcomes. I could get the training right, for example, and select the team I considered to be strongest for the next match. What I couldn't worry about or control was the winning or losing. The result would take care of itself.

My role was to make sure the team performed to the best of their abilities. The way we played, I told myself, would be a consequence of the way we trained. Breaking it down further, the way we trained would be shaped by a disciplined routine including proper sleep, diet and recovery times. These were all elements that could be controlled, and when I concentrated on that my sense of calm and focus returned. Slowly, my confidence increased, which allowed me to recognise my strengths as a manager and keep learning from the experience.

Combat Catastrophising

One effective way to stop fearing the worst is to set down your challenge in writing, as well as all the concerns that have sprung from it. By putting our worries into words, we can quickly see they have led to an imaginary catastrophe. Then we can figure out the actions required to return to reality and regain control of the situation.

Worry
I haven't done my homework on time.

Countdown to catastrophe
1   I'll get into trouble with my teacher.
2   I'll receive a detention.
3   It'll be reflected in my end of term report.
4   My projected grades will be reduced.
5   I'll never get good exam results.
6   My life is ruined.

Deal with it
Talk to your teacher at the earliest opportunity. Take full responsibility for not delivering your homework on time, request

an extension and make sure you keep to your promise. At the very least, your teacher will be impressed by how you handled the situation, and hopefully you'll find an outcome that's acceptable for all involved.

Worry
Instead of starting next week's school football match, I've been put on the substitutes bench.

Countdown to catastrophe
1   The player replacing me is bound to be much better.
2   The team will do fine without me.
3   Maybe I've been holding them back?
4   I'll spend the whole game on the subs bench.
5   I probably won't even make the bench next time.
6   My hopes of becoming an apprentice footballer are finished.

Deal with it
Finding your place on any team is all about making yourself selectable. This means delivering what the coach or manager is looking for. If in doubt, find a quiet time and speak to them. Find out what areas of your performance you need to focus on, and work at them. A positive attitude will always make a strong impression. All being well, you'll look back on this episode as the moment you raised your game and delivered on your potential.

Whether we're feeling worried under pressure, or stressing out about a worst-case scenario, concentrating on controllables will help to restore our focus on the task at hand. When we have the confidence to accept the elements that we can't change or influence, we become free to commit to those we can.

This doesn't just apply to the things that lie directly between us and achieving our goal. Sometimes, the noise around us can undermine our confidence. Whether it's a football crowd or chatter on social media, they're out of our control and can quickly become a negative force. That depends on how we respond to the noise, of course, but personally I find it more effective to focus on what I know needs to be done. As a manager, if I listened to every opinion online it would affect my judgement, and so I respectfully keep my distance. It's an individual choice, of course, but we all have to ask what's more important: pursuing our goal, or seeking to please people on the sidelines? There's no doubt that the technology at our fingertips allows us to connect with people who can help us on our journeys. Just be mindful that if it attracts negativity or unhelpful criticism then it's always in our power to step away or limit what we share.

Ultimately, a focus on controllables can help to create order in our minds, as well as a sense that we can achieve whatever we're setting out to do. With that comes the calm we need to perform at our very best.

SUMMARY

We've come a long way in our bid to demonstrate that anything is possible. First we've had to find the courage to undertake the journey, having recognised what's involved and also believing in our potential to succeed. Then we've looked at the personal qualities we need to take on any challenge, which all comes down to the positive values from being kind at heart.

As we prepare to make a difference to our lives, we've learned how a calm and focused outlook under pressure can prevent our thoughts from racing out of control. Now we're ready to take on anything from small goals to big dreams. Even if we fail at first and then go again, we know that what lies ahead is an experience that will teach us valuable lessons for life.

'SO, CONGRATULATIONS FOR HAVING COME THIS FAR AND COMPLETING YOUR INNER JOURNEY. NOW THE ADVENTURE BEGINS.'

FOLLOW YOUR DREAMS

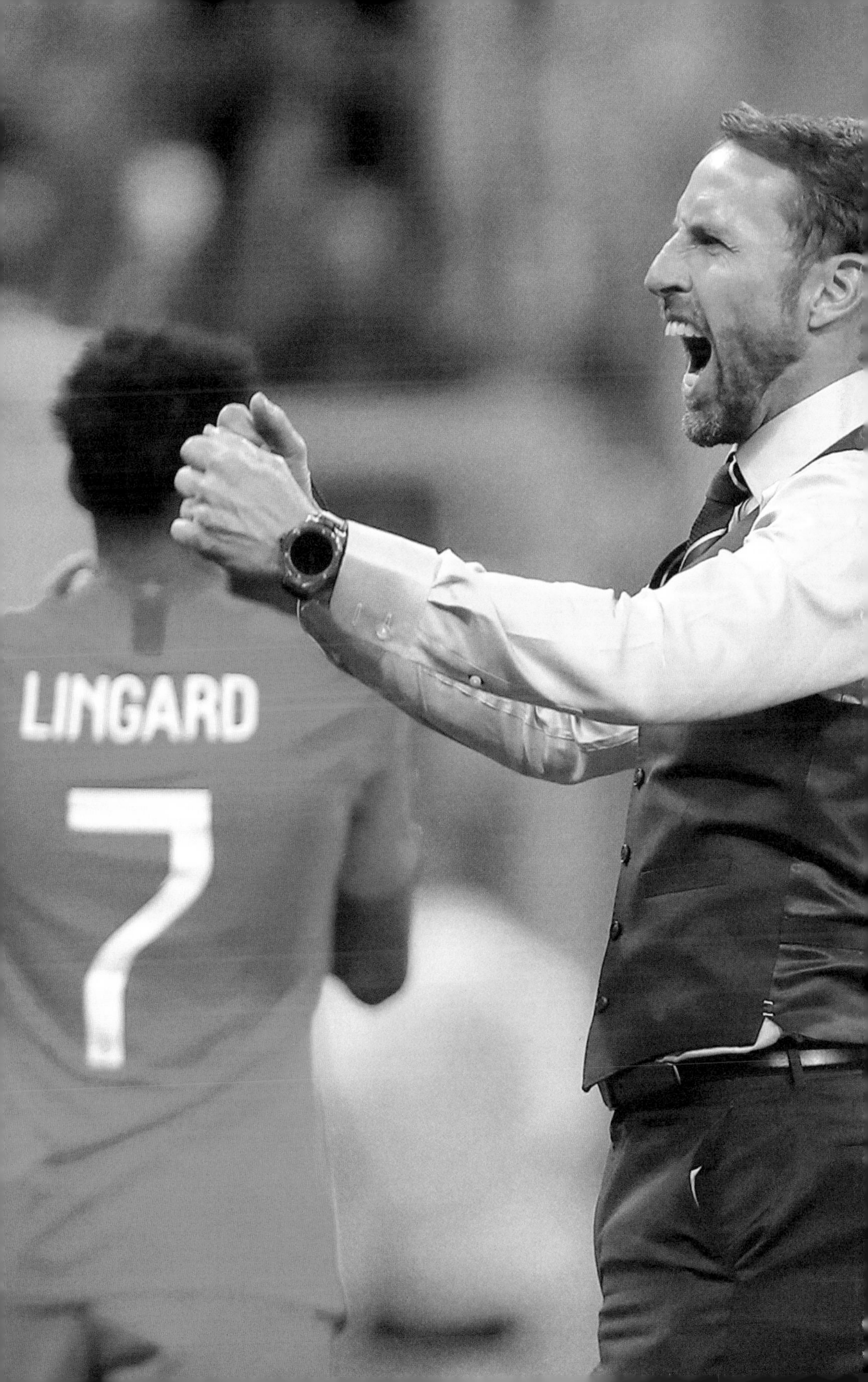
LINGARD
7

We all have a story to tell in life. It's just down to each of us to decide what it's going to be about. We have to ask ourselves if we want to follow an easy path, or take on challenges and discover that we're capable of more than we think.

When I first dreamed of playing football for England, while kicking a football around as a boy in the back garden, I had no idea of what it would take to make it happen. This is an experience most of us go through when we first sense that fire inside us to do something with our lives. It's about passion, pure and simple – and that's the element that encourages us to dream big. It's exciting, after all. Thinking we have the potential to become really exceptional at something can be the motivating force that helps us to get out and train, run that extra mile or practise an instrument for longer.

From there on out, what matters is that we keep that fire burning when reality kicks in and the going gets tough. That means learning to be bold in our outlook, while also holding ourselves to a high standard with kindness at heart. It's the surest way to tackle one hurdle after another in what could be a long, challenging but rewarding journey.

By now, some of you might have found a goal to pursue. It could be out of this world in scale, or just a small change to improve your life. At the same time, if you don't have anything in mind yet, that's fine! A big part of the journey is about understanding yourself, building your confidence along with a positive mindset. That way, you're prepared to take on any challenge when it arises – now, or at any time in the future.

So, let's look at the practical steps to take when the time feels right. It's an exciting moment, and with careful planning and the right support there's every chance that your dream will become a reality.

The
Place
to
Be

Before I left school for the apprenticeship at Crystal Palace, I knew I had to do my best in my exams. My mum spelled out how important it was to gain some qualifications - just in case football didn't work out - and I knew she was right.

Like so many students in the build-up to exams, I spent a lot of time revising in my bedroom. This was the place where I could close the door and concentrate; it gave me space with my schoolbooks, away from all distractions. My bedroom became my base - my revision headquarters. It was the springboard for my attempt to get good grades before pursuing a career in the sport I loved.

After my exams, the Palace training ground served the same purpose. It was where I went to join other young players with potential in getting better at the game. With the coaching on offer, and the chance it gave me to observe older players, this was the place I had to be if I wanted to become a professional footballer. Even though I had to catch two trains on each journey there and back every day, it was worth it. Why? Because it gave me all the tools and support I needed to make my dream come true.

This Is Where It Begins

When it comes to chasing any goal, we all need that one special place where we can focus on the task at hand. Where that place is depends on the nature of the challenge. Learning how to cook the best curry ever might be possible at home in the kitchen, for example, but if we plan to get to grips with a surfboard we're going to need some waves!

Even if we're pursuing projects at home, sometimes the space we need might not be so easy to find. A shared bedroom or a noisy household, for example, can make it hard for anyone to concentrate. In the same way, a challenge requiring special equipment or tutoring, or even an entire team, might mean the place we require for practice is limited by distance, cost or time. We can get to grips with playing the trumpet at home, for example, but rehearsing with an orchestra requires a whole new level of planning.

Everyone has different needs when it comes to fulfilling their dream, of course, but one thing is for sure: with determination, flexibility and creativity, the space to achieve it is out there somewhere. We just might have to create it for ourselves.

Whether it's a boxing gym or a swimming pool, a school library or even an empty classroom, it's down to each of us to identify and embrace the place that helps us to perform to the best of our abilities. It could be a private or shared space, indoors or outside. Even if we can't get to it as much as we'd like, we can still make sure that every moment counts when we're there. What matters is that we feel safe and comfortable in this place, and able to concentrate on becoming the best that we can be.

My Dream Place

To help pinpoint what kind of environment you need to make great things happen, pick three must-have elements from the list below that can help you transform an ordinary space into an extraordinary place. You'll also find space to write down your own requirements if you have something special in mind.

Quiet
Silent
Bustling
Free
Affordable
Inspirational
Practical
Informative
Supportive
Creative
Challenging
Energetic

....

....

....

I Need Space!

There are lots of goals in life that we can't practically pursue from home or school. We're talking about the kind of ambition that requires so much more than time to ourselves at the kitchen table. Many group sports take place on fields, courts and pitches, for example, while clubs and courses are often hosted in halls and public buildings.

If getting there by yourself isn't possible – by foot or by bike – that's when you need to call upon the support of others to help out. It might mean asking a family member to drive you, organising a ride-share with someone else or figuring out public transport. Whatever the case, it pays to work out any travel issues well in advance.

This is about managing your time responsibly. If you're reliant on someone else to quite literally help you go places, then don't leave it until the last minute to sort it out. Instead, find a good time to talk through your options. By showing consideration for others here – especially if you're asking them to give up time for you – then they can only respond constructively to your request. By showing a positive attitude people will want to help.

Travelling to a training ground or club might seem like a chore, but it does create a healthy division between your passion and ordinary life. When I first started out playing football, I had my dad to drive me to and from training or matches. Without his support in those early years, my dream would have stayed in the garden as I kicked a ball about on my own. Even though it meant spending a lot of time in the car, I found those journeys to be useful. When we set out, it gave me a chance to focus my mind on what lay ahead. On the return trip, often chatting with my dad, I had the opportunity to review how things had gone. As a result, I was in the right frame of mind to make the most of my time on the football pitch, and had an opportunity afterwards to process lessons learned.

Strike the Right Balance

It's great to be fired up by a challenge, but we also need some time out to rest and recover. This can be difficult if you're able to pursue your goal from home because, while it can be convenient, it also requires careful management.

If you're making music in your bedroom, for example, that passion can quickly consume all of your time. The trouble is chasing any dream day and night can lead to burnout, which can have a negative effect on the quality of your work. What's more, you risk neglecting other important aspects of your life - from schoolwork and exercise to time with family and friends.

- **Create boundaries.** Chasing a goal from your laptop might seem really convenient, but it can make it hard to put down. Aim to work from one place in particular, so you can walk away when you need some time away.

- **Set up a timetable.** Quality over quantity is key to pursuing a challenge. Half an hour of focused revision is more effective than six hours' clock-watching at your desk.

- **Build in breaks.** Focus, attention and quality of work all improve with regular time out from your task. Viewing a break as a reward for effort can also be an effective motivator. Doing something constructive with your planned time out, even if it's just getting some fresh air, means you're likely to return feeling refreshed.

Space to Think, Room to Talk

As well as establishing a physical place to pursue a goal, it's important to create the mental space we need to process how it's all going. As a schoolboy footballer, I could think during the journeys to and from the training ground with my dad. Later, I used my time on the train travelling to and from my apprenticeship at Crystal Palace in the same way. Instead of staring out of the window, thinking of nothing in particular, I was able to spend those journeys preparing for the day ahead or reflecting on what I'd done.

No matter what our goal in life, we can all benefit from taking some time to ourselves in order to review and assess our progress, identify any setbacks and take lessons from our recent experiences. We don't need a car or train journey to do this, of course. Any quiet place - from the bus stop to the bath - provides a good opportunity to consider the state of play. By making the most of that time with our thoughts, wherever it may be, we can come away feeling like we're in control of our journey to success - rather than just a passenger.

Talking is another effective means of making sense of our progress. Sometimes we might face an obstacle that just seems too hard to overcome, only to find a way over it by putting the problem into words. Opening up to someone familiar with the challenge we've taken on can also work wonders here, whether that's a family member, trusted friend, tutor, team member or coach. At the very least, it's comforting to know there's someone who will always provide a listening ear when we need it.

Famous Spaces

It's always good to find a place that can help you to completely focus on your passion. Even the most unusual locations can be perfect for people to seek inspiration, find their energy or become masters of their craft. As the choices made by some famous names below demonstrate, often it's down to whatever works for you.

- **Serena Williams:** Together with her older sister Venus, Serena Williams spent a great deal of her childhood at the local tennis court in Compton, Los Angeles. Starting at just three years old, under the watchful eye of their father and coach, Serena spent several hours every day practising her skills to perfection.

- **Roald Dahl:** The author wrote many of his most famous works, including *Charlie and the Chocolate Factory* and *Matilda*, from an armchair in his garden shed.

- **Billie Eilish:** The American singer-songwriter recorded many of her early songs with her older brother in his bedroom at the family's home. The pair credit this cramped creative hub for helping them build her distinctive sound.

- **Jean-Michel Basquiat:** The New York graffiti artist started out in the streets in the 1970s, and went on to display his work in art galleries around the world.

- **Neymar:** The Brazilian soccer star claims his childhood spent playing futsal helped him to master his quick-footed skills. A form of football that is popular in urban areas of South America, this fast-moving game is often played on a hard court with five players per side.

- **The Foo Fighters:** In 2010, after playing sell-out gigs in stadiums around the world, Dave Grohl and his band went back to basics by retreating to his garage to record their number-one album, *Wasting Light*.

SUMMARY

We know that breaking down any challenge makes it manageable. It's one thing aspiring to be an astronaut, but in order to reach a destination which literally involves reaching for the stars, we need a plan of action (see page 208).

Once we break it down into the different stages required in order to get there, we can adopt a more realistic approach to the challenge. Then it's a question of taking one step at a time, but also making sure that every step counts. We can't just show up in science class and sit at the back dreaming about walking on the moon. We have to make an effort, engage and ask questions. So, if the classroom is the place to be, we need to make the most of it. There's no time to let our concentration wander, or even fool around. We'd just be cheating ourselves out of an opportunity.

The same goes for any place that allows us to devote our time to mastering our chosen task, whether it's the rugby pitch or the science lab. Once we're in that environment, nothing else matters. We need to devote our time and energy to our passion and make every moment count. Yes, there's always room to joke around and have a laugh, but it's better to earn that lighter moment through working hard first. That's the surest way to get the most out of anywhere that's designed to help us reach our goal.

As our journey progresses, there might be more than one place we need to be to achieve our dreams. By the time a professional footballer retires, they'll have played on countless different pitches, from school grounds to national stadiums, but the approach is

always the same. From the moment that player steps out onto the turf - for a game or training session, at any age or level - they are there to play with their heart and soul.

The same goes for any challenge we've set ourselves. Once we're in the environment we might come to consider as a second home - whether it's the rehearsal room with a band or the library with our textbooks or the hospital ward as a student doctor - we are there to learn, improve and shine.

Team Up With a Mentor

Our teachers at school have knowledge to share. Their role is to guide us on our journey and equip us with the skills we need in order to learn and better understand ourselves, as well as the world around us.

In classrooms, a teacher is easy to spot. They tend to stand at the front, addressing the room, set and collect homework, and also make themselves available on parents' evenings to assess our progress. As students, sometimes we take teachers for granted. *It's just their job*, we think, and then leave school for the real world. Often it's only then that we come to truly appreciate what a remarkable job they've done.

Without their encouragement, patience and guidance – even if we didn't recognise it at the time – we would struggle to believe that we can learn new skills or successfully face challenges. Their role in our lives might be over, but their impact will last a lifetime.

Then there are the teachers we find beyond the classroom. They might not even be aware of their role, and yet they can have a massive influence on us. They could be anyone we like or admire who has experience in overcoming the kind of challenge we've set for ourselves. We're talking about any individual who believes in us, and who we turn to for advice, guidance and support. We take on board their suggestions for improvement, because we know they can help us to achieve our goals.

These are our trusted advisors. We call them our *mentors*.

You Are Not Alone

A mentor is the kind of person who is there for us when we need guidance. In facing any kind of challenge, that moment often arrives when we're questioning if we'll ever succeed.

Back in my time as an apprentice at Crystal Palace, I hit rock bottom when my coach, Alan Smith, called me in and suggested I should consider becoming a travel agent. I was devastated, and struggled to hide it after leaving Alan's office, which was when one of the older players took pity on me. His name was Gary O'Reilly. He was a talented player who had played for Tottenham Hotspur and Brighton & Hove Albion. We lived near each other in Crawley, and as he had a car he offered to give me a lift home. I looked up to Gary, and admired the way he'd found his place in the team. Like me, he was quite a thoughtful and sensitive individual. As I saw things, he didn't fit naturally with the cool gang in the squad but was still popular and admired.

Aware that I was upset, Gary talked to me all the way home. It was clear to me that he recognised I had the potential to be a good player, but needed an education about how football worked. He explained how coaches were always looking for certain things in a player to complement the squad. If I wanted to make myself selectable, he advised me, then I needed to deliver what the coach wanted to see for the benefit of the team while also retaining my own strengths, qualities and character. By the time he dropped me off at home, I felt much more positive about my future in football as a player.

I may not have realised it at the time, but as I look back now at the kindness Gary O'Reilly showed me, I consider him to be an important mentor in my career.

This may come as a surprise, but the other person who I think of in the same way is the youth coach who suggested I'd be better off selling holidays! Alan Smith had my best interests at heart when he called me in to say I'd been dropped. He believed in me, but needed to see me rise to the challenge and fulfil my potential. Like many coaches in that era of football, he was quick to voice his displeasure if a player or the team performed badly. At the same time, he was also the first person to say to me that one day I could play for England.

Alan cared. He treated his players as people and wanted the very best for them. He also came from a successful business background. Sometimes in the afternoons after training he would invite me to get involved in that side of his work, and I would find myself measuring up shops he owned. It was all about gaining a wide range of experience - not just on the pitch, but off it too. Alan Smith saw each player as so much more than just a footballer, and I responded to that.

I still speak to Alan now, more than thirty years on, and value his insight and opinion. He and Gary took very different approaches to helping me find my feet when I needed it, but as mentors, both of them enabled me to tread a difficult path in my early years as a footballer.

'FIND A MENTOR, A PERSON WHO CAN BE THERE FOR YOU WHEN YOU NEED GUIDANCE.'

Mentors Made Simple

- Think of a mentor as anyone we look up to who can help us on our journey.

- In movies, a mentor is often a wise old man or woman, like Gandalf in *The Lord of the Rings*, Obi-Wan Kenobi in *Star Wars*, or Glinda the Good Witch in *The Wizard of Oz*.

- In real life, a mentor could be a team coach or captain, a good friend who understands what makes us tick, or just someone with the experience to help us on our journey.

- A mentor can sometimes offer hard truths. These are insights or observations about our performance that may be difficult or uncomfortable for us to accept, but which we have to act on if we want to succeed.

What Makes a Good Mentor?

Unlike schoolteachers, a mentor isn't a conventional job. Many people who provide insight and guidance might not even realise the impact they are having. So, as we don't generally interview people for the role of mentor, how do we know when we've found someone who can help us on our journey?

Finding the right mentor often depends on our personality, and how positively we respond to guidance and insight. Some people thrive on being told bluntly that they need to improve or risk failure, while others might thrive with a gentler approach. It really is down to individual choice, and what kind of support is needed - and on offer.

Here are some qualities that make a good mentor. Circle three that would appeal to you most in someone you could turn to for guidance and advice:

Friendly

Respectful

Sensitive

Straightforward

Inspirational

Enthusiastic

Honest

Transparent

Motivating

A mentor might be there from the very start of our journey and available at all times, such as a parent or sibling. Others might serve as mentors for a short period or to get us over a particular challenge or hurdle, as I experienced when Gary O'Reilly spelled out the reality of life as a footballer to me. As for Alan Smith's role as a mentor, that became a friendship that will last a lifetime.

Alan and Gary mentored me in very different ways, but I had a huge amount of respect for them both. I looked up to them and valued their opinions, which is essential when it comes to someone who is helping you to achieve your goals. A mentor needs to be able to tell you things that might be difficult, challenging or even upsetting to hear, as they ultimately want you to overcome whatever stands between you and success.

As a schoolboy footballer, I didn't like it when a coach told me I needed to work on my right foot. I'd think they were mistaken or even feel angry, and I'd have to get over that before accepting that they were right. What's more, the coach only offered that advice because he believed that I could do better. As well as believing in you, a good mentor will understand you, and know what it takes to help you tap into your full potential.

MARK ZUCKERBERG

STEVE JOBS

In short, a mentor is a vital source of
wisdom and support on your journey.
They can even help provide
a road map to show you
the way ahead.

Anyone who has ever
experienced success will be
able to name somebody they
turned to for advice. Facebook
creator Mark Zuckerberg credits
Apple's late chief, Steve Jobs, as his
mentor early in the development of his
social network. Five-time Paralympic gold

**PEP GUARDIOLA
& LIONEL MESSI**

medallist Ellie Simmonds was just eleven when she teamed up with her
mentor and coach Billy Pye, an ex-miner and schoolteacher. Lionel Messi
considers his former manager Pep Guardiola to have been key to his
development during their time together at Barcelona; while the musician
Lorde has enjoyed the support of the legendary Elton John.

LORDE

ELTON JOHN

A good mentor can be invaluable, but it's vital that we don't turn to people we respect and admire just to hear what we want. It's always nice to get confirmation that we're doing well, but is receiving nothing but praise really that useful? If that's all we want to hear, then really we need to work on our confidence. It's natural to hit moments of uncertainty as we face a new challenge, but deep down we have to believe in ourselves.

In a similar way, if someone is only being positive because they're worried the truth will hurt, or reluctant to offer criticism because it feels awkward, then we could just drift into failure. That person might mean well, but that doesn't help us to improve.

Then there's the temptation to listen to anyone who offers an opinion. This is often the quickest way to turn any challenge into a mess. The fact is everyone will have something different to say, and some of them will have strong views – and if we try to take them all on board, we lose all structure and focus. We risk becoming distracted by things that aren't important, and we might even lose sight of our long-term goal.

In my role as England manager there are so many voices I could listen to about who should be selected for the team. If I paid attention to them all, my brain just wouldn't cope and I'd be doubting every decision I made. That's why it's so important to build trust with select individuals who offer insight and advice we consider to be valuable. We need to feel sure they're being honest, just as they have to know that we're resilient enough to respond to their input positively. As for criticism that can help us to develop, a good mentor will always find ways to make it constructive.

ELLIE SIMMONDS

Constructive Criticism: Cracked

A critic is someone who judges performance – from sport to the arts, everyone has a right to an opinion. Sometimes that insight can be informative. A review, which is a form of criticism, can help us to see things in a new light. It might provide us with a deeper understanding of a movie, book or video game, for example, while listening to football pundits reflect on a match we've just watched can give us expert insight into tactics or the quality of play.

But then there's the kind of criticism that we might consider to be unhelpful. Often, this is when someone makes a negative comment about something without suggesting ways they believe it could be better. When our own efforts receive purely negative criticism, it can be hard to process. We might feel like we've done the best we can, and so this kind of feedback risks causing confusion and can even undermine future efforts.

That's why the most effective critic is one who is constructive in their approach. We're talking here about someone who recognises our strengths, and views our weaknesses as areas that can be improved. Let's look at some examples of how unhelpful comments can be transformed into constructive criticism:

'That shot was miles off!' ✗

'Look up and you're more likely to shoot on target.' ✔

'You'll never make the squad!' ✗

'If you work hard next season, you could make yourself selectable.' ✔

'Were you asleep when the ball landed in the box?' ✗

'Be more alert for the long ball, and you could score.' ✔

One effective way of recognising constructive criticism is by learning to offer it ourselves. It's a question of finding the positive in anything we review or assess – even if it's only potential – along with steps that the individual or team could take to achieve it. Sometimes that person or group may be experienced enough to know what has to be done, without it being spelled out. Either way, by framing our criticism positively we can be honest about weaknesses and use them as a springboard for improvement. To be sure we're offering constructive criticism, a simple test is to ask ourselves how we'd respond if it was offered to us. Even if it contains hard truths, it has to be advice and insight we can act on to get better. If we can give constructive criticism as well as accept it, everyone shines.

SUMMARY

We know that we are never alone when it comes to facing any challenge. Even if we're pursuing a goal on our own, we all have a team of some sort that we can count on for support. It might be a sibling at home, who's aware that we're upstairs revising hard, or a teacher at school. In sport, it could be a parent or carer who gives us a lift to training or cheers from the sidelines during a match. That support all adds up - we know they want us to succeed, and will do what they can to help. We can count on them when we need it most.

A mentor offers a deeper level of support. This is someone who believes in us as much as anyone else on our team does. The difference is they can see what needs to be done if we're going to progress, and know how to communicate that effectively.

Picking our critics is key here. What we're looking for is a trusted advisor. This is someone who understands us and the challenges we face, and can provide appropriate insight, guidance and advice to help us achieve our goal. A mentor doesn't have to be an expert in the field. They just need to understand what makes us tick and constantly push us towards fulfilling our potential.

A good mentor isn't there just to offer praise when we do well, though no doubt they'll celebrate the high points with us. Their role is to identify where we can do better, and remind us that we have what it takes to overcome any obstacle. A mentor is on our wavelength, and they're a powerful force who is with us in spirit every step of the way.

A Plan of Action

Before starting any journey, we need to know where we're heading. We could just set off and see where the road takes us, but without some direction we'd soon be lost. At the very least, we need to know our destination. How we get there is a matter of choice.

Some people like to know the precise route. They plot it out in advance, figuring out how long it'll take and what time they'll arrive. Others prefer a more relaxed approach. They might take a moment to work out the best way, and then they'll head out with a view to enjoying the journey. They might even take the occasional wrong turn, but will always find their way back onto the right path. In time, they'll get to wherever they want to be.

Then there are those who completely change their plans as they go. They might pass a place that grabs their attention and decide to check it out. As a result, they end up finding somewhere unexpected but more exciting than their original destination. They might choose to stay, and that's completely fine. In every case, the only way to make such a discovery is by setting out on the journey in the first place.

We could be talking about road trips here, but the same approach applies to journeys that involve taking on a new task or challenge. How we choose to get there is down to each and every one of us. In every case, however, we need to at least consider the route. That way, we can always be sure we're heading in the right direction.

So, let's look at what's involved in plotting a route to turn a dream into reality. How do we break down a journey into manageable sections and feel sure we're always on the best path?

Even when we're excited about getting going, it's worth pausing for thought. Why? Because a road map gives us confidence. With a little planning, we can enjoy the journey no matter how we choose to get there.

The Right Direction

I like to know where I'm going. In all the projects and teams I've been involved with, we've had success when we're clear about what we're trying to achieve.

Before we can plan, however, we need a vision. The dream has to come first - it's what starts the fire inside us. It's exciting. In some ways, it's the fuel for our journey. Only once we've got a destination in mind can we focus our attention on how we're going to get there.

Elon Musk is a great example of someone with tremendous drive. His company, SpaceX, is responsible for the world's first reusable rocket. This has huge potential for delivering satellites into Earth's orbit, because it dramatically cuts down on costs. It also brings Musk one step closer to achieving his grand vision of putting human beings on Mars. That is his destination. It might take decades to get there, with each technological breakthrough leading to another until we have the ability to step onto the red planet.

It should be said that there are no rules when it comes to planning. Some people stumble into great things. It's just that relying on that approach can make things harder than necessary. It's difficult to summon the drive to

achieve a goal if we're unsure about how to get there - or even where we're going. That's why it always pays to consider that path before we set off.

So, whatever our goal or ambition - from making a difference to our local community, to becoming an astronaut on the first mission to Mars - creating a plan can only bring us confidence. It means we can set off feeling sure of our direction. Even if the goal itself is so far off it's hard to imagine, a plan means we can focus on taking one step at a time in the right direction.

Let's Make a Plan

These pages are an opportunity to put our dreams down on paper. When a big idea is floating around in our heads, it can be hard to pin down exactly what we want to do with it. Putting the idea into words gives us something to focus on - and can even help sharpen it up until our destination is clear for all to see.

Then, we can start to create a plan to turn that dream into reality.

1. Define your goal

This is your space to work out exactly what dream you want to make possible - no matter how big or personal. Aim to sum it up in a few words if you can. Keeping it simple can help you make the goal more focused.

It might take a couple of attempts before it feels right. Just don't hold back. Even if your ambition feels out of reach right now, with a plan you can make anything possible.

Earn a place in the first team

Start a street photography blog

Ace my science exams

Learn to kite-surf

Complete the Duke of Edinburgh's Award

Become a DJ

Improve my front crawl

Save the planet

Writing down our goal frees up thinking space. Seeing it on paper is the first step towards making it real. Defining our ultimate goal in this way also allows us to turn our attention to the next step, which is all about working out how to make it happen.

Redecorate my bedroom

Get better at Spanish

Go to law school

Stay out of trouble

Your Goal

....

....

....

....

....

....

Find a holiday job

Make a difference

Become a vet

2. Break it down

If we set off on a long trip by car, we'll often stop along the way. A short break is a chance for everyone to stretch their legs and then return to the road feeling refreshed and refocused.

This approach isn't just useful for a car journey. We can do the same thing on the way to making any dream or ambition come true. Sometimes the destination can seem way off in the distance, or almost too difficult to reach. In every case, breaking the journey into stages can make it manageable.

Having identified your destination – or long-term goal – now is the time to look at how to get there by establishing your short- and medium-term goals. Check out the examples across the page, before using the space to work out your own way ahead.

My long-term goal	Become a doctor
My medium-term goal	Study medicine at university
My short-term goal	Get the right GCSEs and A levels

My long-term goal	Represent Team GB at the Olympics
My medium-term goal	Compete at a national level
My short-term goal	Work with a coach

My long-term goal	Save local woodland from development
My medium-term goal	Set up a pressure group
My short-term goal	Get informed about the facts/make contacts

My long-term goal	....
My medium-term goal	....
My short-term goal	....

3. Go deeper

Now you have your long, medium and short-term goals, it's time to break each one down even further. This is where things become practical, and you can start to see how to reach each stage and milestone on your journey.

Taking each goal in turn, take the time now to detail the steps required to make them happen. Then all that's left to do is work out how long the journey is going to last. Much depends on the destination, of course. And in cases where it's not possible to put an exact deadline on achieving some of the steps, an estimate or more general timeframe will work just as well.

In putting together a timeline, the key is not to put yourself under unnecessary pressure. Rushing to achieve something increases the risk of failure, so allow for setbacks and unexpected learning opportunities - and build in plenty of breaks so you can keep a good balance in your life.

		Timeline
My Long-Term Goal	**Become an Actor**	One day!
Steps to take	Find an acting agent	Next autumn
	Make myself available for castings	Next July/Aug
	Sort holiday work for travel costs	Next July/Aug
My Medium-Term Goal	**Be part of a local theatre production**	Next June
Steps to take	Learn to work with a director	Next May
	Get involved behind the scenes	Next Spring
	Join a local theatre group	New Year
My Short-Term Goal	**Appear in the school play**	December 10
Steps to take	Make costume	By December 5
	Rehearse	November 1-30
	Audition	October 15

Review and Improve

It's important to build some flexibility into your plan. This allows for faster progress - and also for any unexpected events or difficulties that may crop up and leave you feeling like you're falling behind.

The way forward is to create regular review periods. By doing this, you'll feel in control while staying focused on your ultimate goal. It isn't just about adjusting the timeline, but also reflecting on what you've learned so far. If it helps, turn to your mentor and chew it over with them. Below is an example of a goal and how the timeline might change.

		Timeline
Medium-term goal	**Charity cycle ride**	~~Sept~~ Nov
Steps to take	Raise £100 in donations	June-~~Aug~~ Sept
Steps to take	Bike training	May-~~Aug~~ Sept

At school, progress is reviewed regularly in the form of a school report. It might feel like a judgement sometimes, but really it's for pupils to check they're on track by measuring where they are now alongside what's possible for them. The report then sets out any improvements that are required to reach that goal. It's a useful collection of data, and what matters is that the pupil acts on it constructively.

In many ways, a school report and a review of our goals are very similar. As we're likely to carry out our own review, honesty is key. There's no point in flattering ourselves when we know in our hearts we could do better. Quite simply it's a chance to look in the mirror and ask searching questions: *Have I put in enough work? Are my behaviours in line with fulfilling my ambitions? Does my plan need adjustment? What needs to be done for me to improve?*

Even if the review highlights work to be done, what matters is the effort we've put in. Whatever we choose to do, hard work and perseverance will help us to improve and see us through, which means never giving up even when the going gets tough.

The Post-Match Review

After England play any game, we always carry out a review. We look at areas in which we performed well, and those we can improve. In order to make it manageable, we break the match into different phases focusing on attacking and defending. The aim is to develop confidence from what we did well, along with a desire to improve the areas that could have been stronger. We'll also look at match statistics so we can be analytical in our review and show clear pathways for improvement. This all helps in providing feedback to the players so they can assess their performance - not just as individuals, but as a team.

My aim is to encourage pride in what we did well, along with a desire to work on our game where we could be stronger. By breaking down the match into markers - or different areas - we are able to be analytical in our review and show clear pathways for improvement.

This way, whether we win or lose, it will always be a learning experience. Whatever the result, it provides us with a way forward, as long as everyone is open to feedback and is focused on playing as a team at the highest level. Should we lose, we aim to work out what went wrong so we can act on it constructively. The wins certainly breed energy and enthusiasm, but rather than sit back feeling satisfied, we see them as an opportunity to challenge ourselves a little more and keep pushing in terms of performance.

As well as reviewing the game we've just played, we'll look ahead to the next one. This is key when we're in a competition such as the European Championship or the World Cup. As a team, it's important that we break our campaign into chunks. We might look at the group stage, for example, in which we face three opponents. We'll look at what we need to achieve in the first match, while also keeping the other two in mind.

We want to win every game, of course, but often it's a question of controlling the pressure we apply to the England team to make sure they deliver every time. This changes as matches take place, depending on how England and our competition fare. Do we need a win, a draw or is it a question of goal difference? Then we'll look at the strengths and weaknesses of the opponent and make sure our attitude to training is spot on, every session. By regularly reviewing all aspects of our game, we know exactly what's required to move forward in what we hope will be our journey to lifting the trophy.

New Pathways

Everyone finds their path in life at different times and in different ways. There is no deadline when it comes to working out our ambitions, and so it's totally fine if things aren't clear just yet. What matters is taking the time to understand ourselves and developing a confident, positive outlook so we can act when the time feels right.

Once we've started on our journey, it's not unusual to come across forks in the path. Another opportunity might open up, and sometimes that can seem like the right path to take. As a boy, I dreamed of becoming a professional footballer. I never once thought I'd be a manager, and yet when the opportunity arose as my playing career came to an end, it seemed like the right thing to do. As a former player, I had insight into how a team responded positively to their coach. Now, I am really fulfilled by the role. I have found that I love helping players achieve their potential, but I would never have made that discovery without enjoying a career on the pitch first.

There are lots of different pathways to achieving a dream, and we are free to plot our own course. The key is to find a path that feels right for you. We can still head for the same destination as other people; it's just we've chosen a route better suited to our skills.

Let's say we're crazy about football but our talents lie off the pitch. We know the England squad isn't just about the players - there's also the staff who play supporting roles. Perhaps our dream job isn't as a striker, but rather as a member of the social media department that makes sure the team stays connected with our supporters. It's a role that can be just as challenging and rewarding, but calls upon different skills. From the analyst to the physio, every member of England's support staff is in the same game as the squad. It's just they've found positions off the pitch where they can excel.

Once we've found our role, we can progress on our journey by playing to our strengths. Often, it takes a diversion in our intended path to be reminded of this. I was once asked to help coach my son's junior football team. As I was a manager at the time, I felt I could at least bring some experience to the role. As it turned out, I struggled to find a way to effectively communicate with players this young. As soon as a match started, they all just got overexcited and flocked around the ball! It was amusing, but it reminded me that my coaching abilities are better suited to working with older players.

My experiences both as a player and as a manager have taught me that there are all sorts of pathways to achieving a dream. We can't all be movie stars, but we can play vital roles behind the scenes in making a Hollywood blockbuster. Ultimately, we're all on the same journey to making the very best film. What's more, every path we take is a valuable learning experience, even if we take a diversion or reach a fork in that path and choose another route.

'EVERY STEP WE TAKE IS PROGRESS. EVEN IF IT DOESN'T FEEL THAT WAY AT THE TIME, THERE WILL ALWAYS COME A MOMENT WHEN AN EXPERIENCE INFORMS OUR NEXT MOVE.'

SUMMARY

Paper and a pen are useful tools when it comes to plotting ways to achieve a dream. Just writing down the big idea in your head is a vital first step towards making it happen. It's also a chance to develop the idea and create that all-important road map.

Some of us might favour a detailed plan, while others are motivated by a sketch. Whatever the case, it's always worth taking the time to think before setting out on your journey. Much like preparing for a trip, you don't want to risk having to turn around when you're halfway there because you've forgotten something vital.

A plan sets out a process. We just need the heart and soul to follow it through. With commitment and positive thinking, the outcome will take care of itself.

Planning can help to minimise drift, encourage focus and create a timeline. It can be something you have to review as you go, but that's fine. Making adjustments keeps you in control. It can keep the dream alive.

Even if your dream is a lifetime in the making, just break it down into manageable stages. Getting to each stage is a reward in its own right, and could even open up other pathways you haven't yet considered.

Whatever goal lies at the end of your journey, there are many ways to reach it. What matters is that you make the effort to get things underway, so you can find the path that suits you down to the ground.

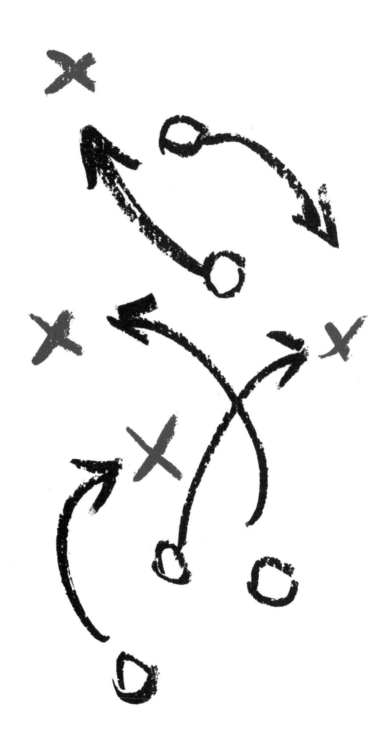

Lows to Highs

Without a doubt, missing the penalty at the Euro '96 semi-final was a low point in my career. I felt I had let everyone down – myself, my teammates and the nation. It wasn't an easy thing to go through, but it turned out to be an important learning experience for me. I became more resilient and bolder in my outlook, because I felt like the worst thing that could have happened was behind me. In many ways, I felt like it helped me to better understand myself. I still wished I had scored, of course, but in time the lessons I took away from that difficult episode were all positive. I don't hide away from what happened. I just learned to take responsibility for how I dealt with it.

When it comes to failure, the reality is that we're not limited to experiencing it just once in life. It can happen many times, and in different ways, and for some it's a necessary pathway to success. That's why it's so important that we're prepared for these moments and able to process them constructively. With the right mindset, failure doesn't mean we're not good enough. It just means we have to try harder next time.

If we work hard at achieving our goals, then at some point we'll experience success. It might sound like one slow climb to the top, but things rarely just become easier. It really is more like a rollercoaster, with a series of ups and downs, twists and turns, and these often happen when we least expect them. Coping with the challenging moments is important, of course, but

there are also issues when it comes to dealing with the high points. Why? Because when we reach the top, the temptation is to sit back - and we all know what follows on that ride . . .

First, let's look at what it takes to turn a low point into a lesson we can't afford to miss. How do we deal with what can be a really difficult time, and come through the other side feeling like it was a useful process?

Learning from Lows

After three years in my role as manager at Middlesbrough FC, I was sacked. I'd had a feeling it might be coming. Having faced relegation from the Premier League the previous season, we had gone through a testing time in the Championship. Even though we'd won the match before I received the news, and the team were climbing towards the top of the table, it felt like change was in the air. After that game, as we left for the changing rooms, some supporters were shouting that I was going to lose my job. It wasn't a pleasant experience.

Then, when I received the news, it just felt like a humiliation. My sacking was almost immediately reported in the media, which made it very public. On the school pick-up run, I felt like everyone was looking at me, and then I had to tell my kids. It was hard not to take it personally, and my self-esteem took a hit. It felt like I had failed in the job.

Then again, I reminded myself, I had been in a similar situation as a player. Having experienced missing a vital penalty, I knew that I could come through this.

Once the shock had passed, my first thought was that my time as a football manager was over. Losing my job in that way was painful, and I didn't want

to risk getting hurt again. I also realised that I had devoted so much of my life to football, both on and off the pitch, that there were lots of experiences I'd missed out on. It had been my life since I was a schoolboy. In my time as a professional footballer, I hadn't been allowed to go skiing because of the risk of broken bones. We also played matches on Boxing Day, and so I had never been away for a family holiday at Christmas. Knowing that I could now enjoy these things came as a comfort. They were small opportunities, but they reminded me that failure is never the end of the road.

I also had one other ambition that I'd never found time to pursue. Running a marathon had always interested me, and this seemed like the perfect opportunity to sign up for a race. It gave me something to focus on, with a training programme and then the challenge of running 26.2 miles. If I hadn't lost my job as manager, this was something that I just wouldn't have done. A small but rewarding opportunity had sprung up from a setback.

While I had no future plans in management, football still opened new doors in my career. I took on television work, sharing my opinion on matches, which I really enjoyed. It gave me a great insight into what goes on behind the cameras, and I worked with interesting people I would never have met as a player or a coach. It also meant I was still involved with the game, but from a refreshing new angle. Even so, I began to miss being able to make a difference to a game from the touchline.

After a few years, an opportunity arose for me to join the FA to focus on youth development. I discovered it gave me a chance to help young players unlock their potential. I became passionate about it, and hungry to learn more. I was aware that I had only found this new interest because I'd been fired as a manager. Now that setback had become a chance to follow a new path in a sport I loved.

When I was given the chance to get back into coaching, by taking on England's under-21 squad, enough time had passed for me to consider it

seriously. I didn't want to get hurt again, but I saw it as a challenge that would put my experience in developing young talent to the test. I hoped I could make a positive contribution, and felt suited to the role. It became my focus, so when I was offered the opportunity to manage England's senior squad in 2016, I turned it down.

It was an honour to be considered, of course, but as well as my commitments to the under-21s, I was frightened of failing in public again. After my experience at Euro '96, and then getting sacked by Middlesbrough, I didn't think the English public would welcome me in the role. So I politely passed on the offer, and it felt like the right decision.

Soon after I'd pushed back on the idea of being a candidate for the job, I was watching a post-match interview with an old Crystal Palace teammate, Chris Coleman, who was the Wales manager at the time. He was celebrating a victory for the team, which was made all the more special because he had previously faced challenges in his career as a coach.

Like me, Chris had been sacked as the manager of a Championship side. The experience had rocked his confidence, and yet he'd found the courage to step up and steer a national team to success. When asked by the interviewer for his advice for anyone in a similar situation, Chris spelled it out very simply: Don't be frightened of going for things in life.

I watched him on the screen, and it felt like he was talking directly to me. I had also been invited to coach a national team, but unlike Chris I'd chosen to back off. Some call managing England 'the impossible job', which makes it sound as if there's no hope of a successful outcome, and I had fallen into that way of thinking. I had become so worried about what could go wrong that I'd failed to consider the opportunities such an honour presented. It had taken watching that interview with an ex-teammate and old friend for me to realise this.

Of course, I also figured it was too late for me to do anything about it. But then the role of England manager became vacant again later that year, just on a temporary basis at first, and I knew what I had to do.

In some ways, having turned down the job once, I felt more confident in my approach. I decided that if I was going to try making a difference, I had to do it in my own way. I knew it could fail, but I wasn't going to worry about that. My focus was on how things might look for the team if it went right.

Looking back, this proved to be one of the most significant decisions in my life. If I think about the worst thing that could've happened, I now know the answer. Had I ruled myself out of the running to become England's senior team coach again, I would've never stopped wondering what might have been.

Instead, committed to growing a young team, my role turned from caretaker to full-time manager, and I have experienced amazing things ever since.

It's an honour to lead the England players; I have enjoyed every moment, and that includes the challenging times. I'm doing what I love, which is helping young players reach the top of their game, and my life would be poorer had I responded to a low point in my career by thinking it was the end of the road. No matter how bleak things become as we pursue our goals, even if it happens a number of times, we can always learn to move on and feel stronger. What's more, that newfound resilience and determination to succeed can help us to climb higher than ever before.

Coping with Rejection

Nobody likes missing out on being selected or an opportunity. It can really hurt, but there are always positives to be gained. Here's how to find them:

1 **Whatever you're feeling is fine.** Rejection can come as a shock. It might even lead to anger and sadness. This is a normal human response. Just don't bottle it up and pretend things are fine if you're struggling. Turn to people you trust, and help make sense of your emotions by talking things through.

2 **Accept the situation.** Eventually, you'll reach a point where you can look back at the rejection without feeling stung. Remember that it wasn't personal. It just came down to the fact that what you had to offer at the time didn't fit the requirements, whether it was for a football team selection process, a job vacancy, or the role of boyfriend or girlfriend if you asked someone out and didn't get the result you'd hoped for! Whatever the circumstances, people will always rate the fact that you had the courage to try.

3. **Recognise your efforts.** Some people can be so fearful of rejection that they avoid circumstances where it might happen. By giving it a shot, you stepped out of your comfort zone, and that should be a source of pride. It didn't work out this time, but you've gained a learning experience.

4. **Ask for feedback.** If appropriate, it's fine to ask for reasons why you were rejected. The key is to be polite when you ask, and equally respectful in your response to any answer.

5. **Learn from the experience.** This is an opportunity to improve. In some ways, it highlights areas to work on - from building confidence to mastering a new skill set. With commitment and determination, you can move on and grow stronger.

6. **Consider your options.** In some cases, you might have the opportunity to step up once again. In others, the fact that one door has closed means others will open. Rejection is never the end. It just leads to options, and you owe it to yourself to choose the path that will allow you to play to your strengths.

Strength from Success

Everyone loves a win. It's a great feeling, and makes the hard work, sacrifice and training worthwhile. It could be the moment a dream becomes a reality, or a stage on the journey where everything has gone right. If you've experienced setbacks and lows in reaching this point, it can feel even sweeter. For some, however, success can create its own challenges, which is why it's good to know in advance how to handle it.

Stay hungry

People who achieve great things are often highly motivated. They can be focused on one goal, and organise their entire life around pursuing it. Then they succeed and find themselves in unknown territory. When you reach the top of your game, how do you stay driven when it seems like there's no further to go?

In sport, successful players can sometimes experience a drop in performance. With nothing to chase and a warm feeling inside from the win, they ease off a little. Rather than getting up at 6 a.m. to train, they might stay in bed for an extra hour. Why? Because in their eyes, they've earned it.

The trouble is there's always going to be someone coming up behind them who is out to seize their crown. Then there's the competitor who lost out last time, who will be extra motivated to succeed. As a result, that champion who had been bathing in glory suddenly finds themselves challenged.

In order for us to stay motivated, the key is to reset our goals. There are many ways to climb the same mountain, after all. What's more, the

challenge of the ascent can be just as rewarding as standing on the summit.

When it comes to building on success and never taking a foot off the throttle, let's look at Lewis Hamilton. He's won multiple Formula One World Championships, and yet each season he returns to the grid with a renewed passion. How? Because after each win he sets his sights on new goals and targets. It could be the number of pole positions or race wins - or even just a detail in pursuit of racing perfection - but it's more than enough to keep Lewis challenging for each championship.

Stay humble

As an apprentice footballer, part of my job involved looking after a senior player's boots. I'd have to clean them after each match until they looked as good as new. Sometimes, I'd even receive a small tip for my efforts. It was all part of a rota for the apprentices that also involved chores like dealing with dirty kit and mopping the dressing room floors. It was hard work, and I hated it!

But it was also an experience that shaped me as a player. Pushing a mop around, I was at the bottom of the football food chain. All I wanted to do was climb to the top. *If I ever have an apprentice to clean my boots, I thought to myself, I'll make sure I tip better than this lot!*

Now the young players are called scholars and aren't required to do the menial jobs. This allows them to focus on learning the game, but I'll never forget how it felt to be the apprentice. It gave me a fantastic grounding, and fed my hunger to make a success of my football career. In many ways, when success came, that experience helped to stop me from taking it for granted.

We all have to start our journeys somewhere. Often, that doesn't amount to much. It might seem frustrating at the time, especially when we look at

how far we have to travel, but it's also a valuable experience. Later, should we be fortunate enough to find success, it serves as a reminder of just how far we've come. That can be a humbling feeling, which can help to keep us grounded - and also motivate us to keep on pushing.

Look beyond fame

It's easy to think of celebrity as a measure of success. People in the public eye appear to have it all, and we can fall into thinking that somehow being famous is the goal. Social media has made it possible to achieve global recognition very quickly, but it's often based on very little substance. Without feeling like we've earned the recognition by being good at something, insecurities and anxiety about our true worth can kick in. As a result, we can develop an unhealthy relationship with fame, and worry that without it we'll be seen to be a failure.

There's no doubt that sometimes fame can be fun. Professional footballers often have to get to grips with it, and for some it can be a buzz. In most cases, however, fame can make it difficult to do everyday things in public. It can also be quite shallow, focusing just on a glamorous lifestyle, for example, which can distract you from the thing that brought you success in the first place.

Fame might bring adulation, but it also invites criticism and judgements that sometimes feel wrong or unfair. It certainly used to affect me early in my career. Sometimes it could seem to me as if everyone had an opinion on my performance on the pitch. It could hurt if a TV or radio commentator came down heavily on me. Through experience, I learned to focus on my own judgement and only listen to my trusted advisors, rather than set out to please my critics. To manage fame constructively, it's important to be able to step back from what can be very negative energy.

Finally, fame doesn't last. Even if we've become successful through hard work, there will always be something or someone else that takes attention

away from us. That's why it's so important not to become attached to fame of any kind. It's nice to be recognised for our achievements, but our true value comes from wanting to be good at whatever we choose to do. That's a feeling that can't be taken away, because we'll always look back at how hard we worked for our achievements, and see them as a source of pride.

SUMMARY

When we take on a challenge, there will always be high points and low moments ahead. It's all part of the journey, like a path over peaks and troughs.

Often, the best way to learn how to manage the good times and the bad is to experience them first hand. It's not always easy, but we can take steps to prepare. This way, when we're faced with unknown territory - like dealing with rejection or sudden fame - we can keep our heads up, stay strong and remain focused.

The fact is that rejection hurts. There's no avoiding the difficult feelings that can come from being told we haven't been selected or made the grade. The key is to process those feelings, rather than pretend they don't exist. They're a natural human response to disappointment. What matters is that we recognise the rejection is not a judgement of our personal worth. It all comes down to meeting certain requirements, such as particular skills or experience, at that moment in time. What's more, even though we've missed out on this occasion, we still have lots to offer - including the courage it took to offer ourselves up for consideration in the first place. These are things to build on, which can help us to move forward positively.

Hopefully, after all the effort we've put into our challenge, we'll find success. This can also be a moment that takes some of us by surprise. We've earned the chance to celebrate, but there may still be work to be done. Footballers are the first to go wild after scoring a goal, and yet there's always time left in the game. They have to move on swiftly from that moment, and keep playing to the best of their abilities.

We can do the same when dealing with high points in any walk of life. By all means take some time out to enjoy the moment, but don't let it distract from what matters most: the pursuit that delivered us here, the fun we had and the friends we made along the way, and the passion that can take us further.

Giving
Back

We all have the potential to make anything possible. It's a gift within each and every one of us. Sadly, we don't always realise this about ourselves.

It's easy to look at people who have made a success of their lives, and feel we can never do the same. All sorts of things can hold us back - a lack of confidence or support, not knowing where to begin, or just a worry about the commitment. Uncertainty about what the future holds can also be a factor, as life with the Coronavirus pandemic has shown us all.

At the same time, no matter what obstacles lie before us, we each have the potential to create opportunities.

Hopefully, this book has shown what it takes to turn a dream into a reality. The qualities are within us all; we just need to tap into them. Even if we feel we're starting at a disadvantage, help is always out there to get us on the right track. It's just a question of reaching out to those who believe in us, sharing everything from our worries to our hopes and ambitions, and then putting in the time and effort to make great things happen.

As we reach this final chapter of the book, it could be that you've already started making plans to tackle a new challenge. Maybe you've even taken the first steps on that journey. Even if you've just been inspired to think about your goals, that's an achievement in itself. Whether you find your calling now or at any time in the future, it is in your power to make the most of life and become the best version of yourself.

What's more, there's every chance that the efforts you make will encourage some people to think about their own potential. It could be a friend who sees the rewards that come from pursuing a passion, or a fellow competitor who's moved by you to up their game. They could be older than you or younger. They might be taking on the same challenge or something in a completely different field. Whatever the case, it's a great feeling to know that your efforts can inspire others.

As we work towards our goals or even achieve them, the opportunity can also arise for us to help others more directly. We know the importance of having a mentor for support, but in time we could find people turning to us for wisdom, guidance and advice.

So, having explored how we can make a difference to our own lives, let's look at how that experience can help us to give back.

Helping Others

As a footballer, I thought nothing could match the satisfaction that comes from playing. Then I retired from the pitch, moved into coaching and took on new challenges. In many ways, by helping young players to shine, I found the experience to be even more rewarding. I'm still involved in the sport I fell in love with as a kid. Back then, I only dreamed about being a player and not a manager and yet I'm just as passionate about the game today. The only difference is that now my commitment is not to playing to the best of my abilities, but to creating a strong team capable of winning.

My mentor Alan Smith once said to me that there is something very satisfying about the pupil becoming the teacher. I can appreciate that now, and see he's right. I thoroughly enjoyed my career on the pitch. Even so, I didn't achieve everything I had hoped for as a player. Looking back,

although I worked as hard as I could, I didn't dream big for some time. I limited my beliefs to what I thought was possible, and it took me quite a while to realise I could play at the top level. That meant I didn't play for England until I was twenty-five. Many of my teammates were much younger, and so they had longer to fulfil their potential as international players.

While I feel I could have got a little bit more out of myself, as a coach I now have the opportunity to help younger players do just that for themselves. Anyone who has been on a journey to achieve a dream has the wisdom of experience on their side. It's a great feeling to share that, so those who are starting out can benefit from it.

In football, we see players brimming with talent at every level. If we can just wrap all the support systems around them then they'll fly, and it's so rewarding to see. The same applies to any pursuit, in fact. Sharing lessons we've learned from our own experiences helps to grow the community around us and encourages a feeling of togetherness. Our insight and advice can be inspirational, and even build confidence in those who might otherwise stay in their comfort zone.

'IN A SMALL WAY, BY HELPING OTHERS TO FULFIL THEIR POTENTIAL, GIVING BACK REALLY CAN MAKE THE WORLD A BETTER PLACE.'

How to Help

If someone asks for your guidance, how can you provide it?
Here are six ways of helping out and making a difference:

1 **Offer a listening ear.** Often, people who like and admire
others for pursuing or achieving a goal just want to talk.
They might wish to share their own dreams, to seek
assurance or ask for advice. You don't need special
qualifications to provide that. Just speak from your own
experience. It can only help you to feel confident in your
response. This way, whatever you have to share will be
useful.

2 **Define their goals.** We've seen how it's good to put an
ambition or target into words. This is your chance to
encourage others to do the same. Helping someone to
establish their aim will provide clarity and help them to
work out the best way forward.

3 **Provide options.** There's no need to tell someone what to
do. Instead, encourage them to take responsibility for their
own decisions. By setting out the choices available, they
can find a way to progress that feels right for them.

4 **Be positive.** Your encouragement will go far. Think how
constructive criticism benefited you, and then apply it to
your own approach when it comes to supporting someone.

5   **Give feedback.** Be honest in a way that enables them to learn from any mistakes. This way, they can take their next steps feeling stronger and wiser for the experience.

6   **Create space.** A good mentor knows when to step back. By doing so, you're allowing that person to spread their wings. By all means make yourself available, but encourage them to come to you should they need your help or advice.

Our journey doesn't have to have come to an end before we can help others. Sometimes, people are drawn to us for advice simply because we've found the courage to chase our dreams. Even if we're a long way off from achieving our goal, we might still have made more progress than others - which means we have valuable experience to share.

At the start of my career, playing with the Crystal Palace youth team, we looked up to the group above us. They were only a year older, but I found that if I was struggling with things, I could talk to them. I learned a lot from my coaches, of course, but my peers helped me in different ways. Sometimes, it was enough just to see that the older players had got through whatever challenge I was facing. That gave me the confidence to follow in their footsteps.

So, if you're ever approached for advice by someone, simply be yourself. That's what has caught their attention and earned their respect and admiration. There's no need to be the world expert. The fact that they've come to you is a sign that you must be doing things right. What's more, you might well find that you can learn from each other.

Skills for Life

If everyone around us appears to know their purpose or calling and we don't, it can feel like we're missing out. It can also pile on the pressure for us to take on a challenge before we're ready, or when our heart isn't in it. That's why the most effective thing we can do is to take the time to understand ourselves first.

When it comes to setting goals, in some cases it's easy to worry that somehow it's a commitment for life. You might set your sights on training to be an engineer, for example, but what happens if you realise halfway through the course that in fact your passion is in design? Is it the end of the world? Have you made a huge mistake?

Far from it. Because the fact is so many of the skills you will have picked up along the way are transferable.

The Transfer List

- A transferable skill is an ability that can prove useful in lots of different roles. Leading a group, communicating within a team or working with others to solve problems are common examples of skills we can use in all walks of life.

- Qualities like resilience and an ability to organise or inspire people are also portable. We can carry them around should our journey take us in an unexpected direction.

- When we start to think about transferable skills, it opens up a whole world of possibilities. It can also help to make the commitment to a particular goal feel less scary.

- Following one path can lead to other opportunities - and by having skills we can carry across with us, we'll always be prepared in some way.

- Transferable skills are also useful when it comes to giving back. If we're experienced in working with others or performing under high pressure, the lessons we've learned will still be useful to someone specialising in a completely different field. A surgeon can learn from an air traffic controller, for example, or a football coach from a motor racing team.

SUMMARY

Across all walks of life - sport, the arts, politics, charity, the military, industry, and all the rest - we rely on the same basic people skills, which are all about how we interact with each other to achieve a positive outcome. We might wear different uniforms, and yet in many ways we could swap jobs and still have a basic understanding of what's involved.

It takes time to master any role, of course, or specialise in a particular area, but it's never too late to reinvent ourselves if that's what we choose to do. Nor is any venture that we leave behind a waste of effort. Each of us grows from experience, which helps us to understand ourselves, the world around us and the people in it. And as we grow, that helps us to give back.

With a bold outlook and kindness at heart, everything we encounter in life is a learning experience, from the goals we set ourselves to the challenges we face and the friends we make - and even help - along the way. We might follow one path, and learn to master a certain role or skill, or find ourselves branching off in a new direction if that's where our passion lies.

In every case, no matter how we choose to fulfil our potential, we can all take the next step beyond this book knowing that the possibilities are endless.

We really can do anything. It's just a question of rising to the challenge.

The Prince's Trust

If you are aged 11 to 30 and live in the UK,
The Prince's Trust can support you to achieve your full
potential. The Prince's Trust offers hundreds of free
courses, grants and mentoring opportunities to inspire
young people from all over the UK to
build their confidence, start a career or launch
their own business.

Visit www.princes-trust.org.uk, and search
Prince's Trust on social media to find out more.

Prince's Trust

NOTES

NOTES

NOTES

1 3 5 7 9 10 8 6 4 2

Century
20 Vauxhall Bridge Road
London SW1V 2SA

Century is part of the Penguin Random House group of companies whose
addresses can be found at global.penguinrandomhouse.com.

Penguin
Random House
UK

First published by Century in 2020

www.penguin.co.uk

Hardback ISBN 9781529135329

Printed and bound by L.E.G.O. S.p.A, Vicenza, Italy
Designed and illustrated by Two Associates

Penguin Random House is committed to a sustainable future for our
business, our readers and our planet. This book is made from Forest
Stewardship Council® certified paper.

FSC
www.fsc.org
MIX
Paper from
responsible sources
FSC® C004592